To: Allas.
Thank you for your
knowledge and thoughtfulness
Dawn

Elite
Etiquette

DAWN BRYAN

ISBN: 1-4792-9098-X
ISBN 13: 978-1-4792-9098-7
Library of Congress Control Number: 2012923351
CreateSpace Independent Publishing Platform
North Charleston, SC

THE WORLD WAS MY OYSTER, BUT I USED THE WRONG FORK.

– Oscar Wilde

To the Memory

of

John J. Casey

Contents

ELITE SOCIAL GRACES:
THE FINER POINTS / 265

PREFACE

*Experience is a hard teacher because she gives the test
first, the lesson afterward*

– Vernon Law

*S*ocial behavior—or etiquette—evolves differently within different
cultures. And "cultural competence" is the learned ability to navi-
gate successfully any situation within that culture. Cross-cultural
awareness—at every level– has become a prerequisite for contemporary business and social interaction.

*Civilizations, countries, communities, and courts—from ancient China
and Greece to pre-revolutionary France and contemporary America—have
developed and imposed rules for proper social conduct. Appropriate behavior is also expected within various recreational activities, clubs, organiza-
tions, religions, celebrations, and interest groups. Their specific protocols
and codes of social behavior are designed to make social relationships run
more smoothly by clarifying how everybody is supposed to act.*

*Although the word "elite" is now used to describe everything from quar-
terbacks and media to credit cards and sedans, it usually means members
of a particular society are considered superior because of their talent, power,
intellect, or wealth. Their recreations, pleasures, and everyday activities are
generally not part of most of our everyday lives. Yet, over time, knowledge
of these traditions has come to represent a person's background, education,*

interests, and status. Often "unvoiced", these customs are both a sign of belonging and a way of expressing respect. Whoever aspires to elevate or strengthen business or social relationships needs to understand the rules, courtesies, and expectations that identify membership in these elite groups.

Elite Etiquette *gives you the information you need to feel comfortable wherever you are. Even if you have never been a spectator at a golf tournament, enjoyed a live opera, sailed on a yacht, attended a Catholic or Jewish wedding or funeral, stomped on a polo field, sliced a truffle, opened a champagne bottle, or eaten a whole artichoke,* Elite Etiquette *explains everything you: Need to Know; May Want to Know; May Find Helpful to Know; Must Not Do.*

"Etiquette" can be tradition-bound and rigidly—though politely—enforced. However, all manners must adapt not only to the times but also to the particular situation. Those seeking social acceptance will welcome changing cultures and unexpected circumstances as an opportunity for personal growth and refinement.

Your new cultural competence will give you the confidence to put others at ease.

ACKNOWLEDGEMENTS

Although tthe factual information here is available, and has been gleaned, from many different places—books, articles, Wikipedia, programs, lectures, clubs and associations—much of the material comes from my own very diverse social and business experience. Here it has been collected and formatted to define quality behaviors within particular cultures. My goal was to help the reader quickly locate those answers and understandings which would give her/him competence and confidence. I thank the many friends and acquaintances who, over the years, have provided information, set examples, offered advice, and supported me—some without even realizing it. Special gratitude to Denise Lalonde for her technical expertise, helpfulness, and heart in bringing this book to life and to Larry Braunstein for his continuing support.

I am truly appreciative of the encouragement received from Paula Conway, James Leary, and Christina Hummer.

Particular thanks to my animal family—Daphne, Zoe, and Petunia—for their ongoing forbearance, patience, and purring. And their insistence on my taking a break for their afternoon play period.

The charming drawings were executed by artist Susan Ackerman. I thank you.

Kevin Anderson and Akiko Yamagata did an exceptional editing and formatting job—comprehensive, thorough, and meticulous. Thank you for your significant contribution.

PART ONE

GUESS WHO'S COMING TO DINNER? DINING DILEMMAS

Formal Dining

At a formal dinner party, the person nearest death should always be seated closest to the bathroom.

–George Carlin

A formal meal is one at which guests are seated at a dining table and are served by others. It may be a catered banquet or a dinner at a private residence or restaurant. The formal meal can include as many as six or seven courses: 1) an appetizer or first course of soup, shellfish, or fruit; 2) a fish course; 3) the entrée or main course, usually served with vegetables; 4) salad; 5) dessert; and 6) coffee and cordials. Sorbet may be served between courses to cleanse the palate, and a cheese course is sometimes added or offered as an option for the dessert course. The success of the event depends on the knowledge of both a hospitable host and a gracious guest.

WHAT YOU NEED TO KNOW

As a Guest

- ❖ Always bring or send a small gift to the host—not one that is expected/obliged to be used for that occasion.

- ❖ If you arrive at a restaurant before your host, wait for your host in the waiting area, not at the table.

- ❖ At a dinner party, wait for the host to sit down before taking your seat, unless you are asked to sit first.

- ❖ Men sit after the women are seated.

- ❖ If a woman arrives late, all the men rise, and the man on her left helps her to be seated.

- ❖ At a restaurant, begin eating after everyone at your table has been served.

- ❖ At a private residence, begin eating when your host picks up a utensil to begin eating.

- ❖ Always use utensils from the "outside in."

- ❖ Use serving utensils, not your personal silverware, to serve yourself.

- ❖ To signal that you have finished a course, rest your fork, tines up, and your knife, blade in, on your plate. The handles should rest on your plate at five o'clock, and the tips should point to ten o'clock.

- ❖ After a formal dinner, send the host a written thank-you note—not a text or an e-mail.

As a Host

- ❖ Whether for business or pleasure, try to invite guests well in advance.

- ❖ If it is a business meal, reconfirm with your guests.

- ❖ Work out seating placements ahead of time. Generally, women are seated according to their ranks to the right and left of the host, and the male guests, are seated according to their ranks to the right and left of the hostess. The place of honor for a special guest or customer is to the right side of the host.

❖ When possible, men and women are seated alternately.

❖ The place setting for a formal table is always arranged geo-metrically—with the centerpiece in center, place settings evenly spaced, and utensils balanced on each side.

❖ If using a charger (service plate), it is removed before the main course is served.

❖ Food is always served from the right, and dishes are removed from the left.

❖ Wine is served from the right prior to each course and replenished as needed.

❖ The server may unobtrusively sweep the table between courses.

FORMAL AND INFORMAL TABLE SETTINGS

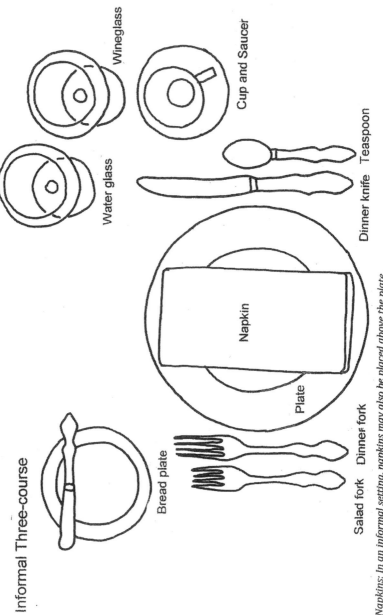

Informal Three-course

Bread plate

Wineglass

Water glass

Cup and Saucer

Teaspoon

Dinner knife

Napkin

Plate

Salad fork   Dinner fork

Napkins: In an informal setting, napkins may also be placed above the plate, in a napkin ring or fancifully arranged in a glass. In a formal setting they may also be placed on the service plate. Placing napkins under utensils can make for an awkward situation

The fourth glass in a formal setting is for sherry or champagne for toasting.

Champagne glass

Wineglass (white)

Wineglass (red)

Water glass

Cup and Saucer

Generally aren't placed on the table until the dessert course

Cocktail fork

Soup spoon

Teaspoon

Dinner knife

Place card

Dessert spoon

Cake fork

Service plate

Formal

Bread plate

Dinner fork

Salad fork

Napkin

Knife blades are always placed with cutting edges toward the plate.

In a formal place setting everything is geometrically placed.

Generally no more than three of the same utensils are placed on the table at the same time; additional utensils are brought with the food. All utensils are placed in order of use.

WHAT YOU MAY WANT TO KNOW

As a Guest

❖ Arriving before the stated time is unacceptable.

❖ As soon as you are seated, remove the napkin from the place setting, unfold it (do not shake it open), and place it on your lap. At some formal restaurants and residences, the server may do this for you. Leave it on your lap until the end of the meal. If you must leave the table, loosely fold it and place it to the left or right of your plate. At the end of the meal, leave it semi-folded to the left of the place setting.

❖ Always join in toasting.

❖ If the server leaves the check in the middle of the table rather than giving it directly to the host, do not reach for it. Allow the person who invited you to pick it up.

❖ When not eating, try to keep your hands in your lap—no slouching or fidgeting.

❖ If you are unable to get a piece of food onto your utensil, use a piece of bread or your knife—not your finger—to push it on.

❖ Although combining condiment with appropriate shaker is controversial, the salt shaker is usually the one with the fewer holes. Checking before vigorously shaking is a good idea.

❖ Pace your eating so that you are not finished before everyone else.

As a Host

❖ Arrange for coats, hats, wraps, etc. to be taken from guests when they arrive or clearly indicate where they should go.

❖ At a private residence, the host (or a designated person) indicates where women should leave their purses.

❖ Make it easy for guests to leave their drinks behind before going in to dinner by having someone collect unfinished drinks or by placing a tray for used glasses in a convenient location.

❖ At a formal dinner, the host enters the dining room first, escorting the female guest of honor.

❖ If there are no placards, the host enters the dining room first to tell guests where to sit.

WHAT YOU MAY FIND HELPFUL TO KNOW

As a Guest

❖ If someone requests the salt or pepper, always pass both together.

❖ If a prayer or blessing is offered before the meal, you may join in or be respectfully silent.

❖ The well-mannered guest usually stays approximately an hour after the dinner ends. If everyone is staying longer and enjoying the evening, feel free to do the same.

❖ If you must leave early, exit discreetly.

❖ For a business meal, if possible, find out whether your guest prefers certain cuisines or enjoys a special restaurant.

❖ Choose a restaurant with a varied menu when hosting a group.

WHAT NOT TO DO

❖ Arrive late.

❖ Bring a cocktail glass to the dinner table.

❖ Change—or ask to change—table assignments or switch name cards.

❖ Request food other than what is being served at a private function.

❖ Bring your purse to the table in a private residence. The host will indicate where to leave it.

❖ Place your purse on the table.

❖ Talk with food in your mouth.

❖ Season your food before tasting it.

❖ Grab a food item, such as a roll, when it is being passed to someone else.

❖ Place your napkin on your chair or plate.

❖ Place a knife, spoon, or fork that you have been using directly onto the table. Rather, place it diagonally on the edge of your plate.

- ❖ Turn your wine glass upside down to indicate that you do not care for any wine.

- ❖ Push your plate away from you at the end of the meal.

- ❖ Criticize the food, room, guests, or host.

Serving and Eating Caviar

Champagne wishes and caviar dreams.
　　　　　–Robin Leach, *Lifestyles of the Rich and Famous*

What You Need to Know

What It Is

Caviar is the processed, salted, unfertilized eggs of fish, most notably the sturgeon, of which there are twenty-seven species.

The labeling of caviar can be very confusing, as some labels refer to the marketing name of the caviar (the eggs), some to the common fish name, and some to the Latin species name. The use of "beluga" and "osetra" are given to many different sturgeon eggs. It therefore behooves the consumer to know something about each of the main species of sturgeon from which caviar is taken. By American and French law, anything labeled simply "caviar" must be sturgeon egg.

Types of True Sturgeon Caviars

- Beluga: Large, glossy, grey to black eggs with a dark spot in the middle and a creamy, buttery taste.

- Osetra: Medium grey to dark brown eggs with a nutty flavor; considered second in quality to beluga.

- Sevruga: Smaller greyish to black eggs; strongest in flavor.

- Sterlet: Small golden eggs with a mild taste.

- Baerii: Small dark eggs with a taste similar to osetra.

- American white sturgeon: Medium brown to black eggs with a buttery taste.

- American lake sturgeon: Comparable in size, color, and taste to beluga caviar.

- American paddlefish: Small to medium grey eggs with an earthy flavor.

- Hackleback: Small black eggs with a nutty flavor.

How to Prepare

- Keep in the refrigerator until ten to fifteen minutes before serving, and open the container immediately before serving.

- Use only glass, wood, gold, or mother-of-pearl spoons and dishes in handling the caviar.

- Be extremely gentle and slow while spooning, lifting out, and spreading.

How to Serve

- Spread a thin film of unsalted butter on lightly toasted bread or on blinis—either as a side if eating caviar straight or with caviar spread on the toast or blini.

- Some non-purists prefer accoutrements such as sour cream, crème fraiche, chopped egg and onion, or a squirt of lemon.

- Other serving suggestions: atop hard-boiled quail or deviled eggs, with raw oysters, or with baked or shredded potatoes.

- If eating caviar straight, allow at least ½ to 1 ounce per person.

How to Keep

- Keep caviar very cold, at 26 to 34 degrees Fahrenheit. Keep in the lowest section of the refrigerator, where it is coldest.

- Once opened, caviar should be consumed within a few days.

- Put plastic wrap over the unused portion before putting the lid on the jar.

- Rotate the tins/jars twice a day to distribute the oils.

- Unopened caviar shelf life in an unpasteurized tin is three weeks; a pasteurized tin is three to four months; and for vacuum-packed containers, read label for shelf life.

WHAT YOU MAY WANT TO KNOW

- To savor, let each egg break against the roof of your mouth slowly.

- Some non-sturgeon caviars must legally have the fish name preceding the word "caviar" on the label. These include lumpfish caviar (tiny eggs dyed black or red); whitefish caviar (small yellow eggs); salmon, or red, caviar (light orange to deep red); carp, or tarama, caviar (orange, often smoked); and rainbow trout caviar (small, orange, and mild).

- Concerns with wild caviar: There has been a devastating decline in all European, Russian and Middle Eastern sturgeon populations because of reduced spawning grounds, pollution, overfishing, poaching, unrestricted domestic consumption, and a lack of enforcement of quotas and bans. Sturgeon do not mature and lay eggs until late in life, and they spawn very infrequently. Thus, without strict controls, eating caviar is not sustainable.

- Aquaculture is producing high-quality, sustainable caviar and is reviving species that were once much more vulnerable.

- The waters in which the fish swim affect caviar. Many consumers are therefore concerned about eating caviar from the Caspian, since that body of water is quite contaminated.

WHAT YOU MAY FIND HELPFUL TO KNOW

◆ Each company has its own labels for different grades. Caviar is graded according to the following criteria: egg uniformity, egg size, egg color, egg maturity, separation of egg grains, fragrance, egg lucidity, and eggshell hardness. Grading caviar requires ten to fifteen years of strictly supervised apprenticeship.

◆ When fresh caviar is packaged correctly at the source, it can remain fresh for a year or more, but once that initial bulk packaging is unsealed and the caviar is put into small tins for sale, it will remain fresh for just a few weeks.

◆ Caviar has a high amount of the neurotransmitter acetylcholine, which increases tolerance to alcohol, thus supposedly decreasing the effects of a hangover.

◆ Caviar is a supposed aphrodisiac because it contains arginine, a vascular dilator that increases blood flow.

◆ Caviar contains forty-seven vitamins and minerals!

◆ Caviar is very high in cholesterol, with 165 milligrams per ounce—that's 55 percent of the daily recommended amount.

◆ Caviar produced in Europe, Russia, and the Middle East often contains borax, which is added to make the eggs firmer and sweeter. Borax is a carcinogen not permitted in food produced in the United States.

◆ When fish are killed in the process of harvesting caviar, there is little waste. The fish meat is sold fresh or smoked and is considered very tasty. There is also a market for other parts of the fish: sturgeon skin is used in making Italian handbags, for example, and Sevruga swim bladders are used to produce isinglass.The actual processing of caviar includes various methods of egg removal, meshing, salting, and packaging.

WHAT NOT TO DO

◆ Freeze caviar. This will destroy the texture and the taste.

◆ Store in the door section of the refrigerator.

◆ Leave caviar exposed to the air for prolonged periods.

- Use silver or stainless steel to serve or eat caviar. Any metal that oxidizes easily will impart a metallic taste to your caviar.

- Serve sour cream, crème fraiche, egg, onion, etc. to caviar purists.

- Never cook fresh or pasteurized caviar, as it will become tough and unappealing. Rather, add it to your recipe at the very last minute—or use solely as garnish.

- Refuse to taste or try it.

LEXICON

BRINING (salting): The process of adding sea salt to the roe. The salt keeps it from freezing at the required storage temperatures while curing the caviar, making it firmer. This is a very sensitive and demanding skill that takes years of experience.

FRESH: The roe are uncooked, have only salt added, and have been processed under optimal refrigeration conditions.

MALOSSOL (lightly salted): When roe is of especially high quality, less salt (not more than 5 percent and often less than 3 percent) is used to allow the native flavors to stand out. But less salt means it is more perishable and thus more expensive.

MESHING: The process of removing extra liquid, filtering out eggs that are too soft, and separating eggs into uniform sizes.

PASTEURIZED: The roe are partially cooked to help preserve them, so they have a longer shelf life and may not even need to be refrigerated (check the label). However, pasteurization changes the flavor and texture slightly, making the eggs firmer.

PRESSED: The roe that is crushed in processing and sold as a jam-like spread, often with several species mixed together. Pressed caviar is often used for cooking.

Pointless…like giving caviar to an elephant.

–William Faulkner

Truffle Etiquette:
Slicing, Shaving, and Serving

There are two types of people who eat truffles: those who
think truffles are good because they are dear and those
who know they are dear because they are good.

–J. L. Vaudoyer

WHAT YOU NEED TO KNOW

What They Are

Truffles are underground mushrooms that form a symbiotic association (mycorrhizae) with the roots of trees. Like mushrooms, they are
only the fruit of the fungus, and only a few of the hundreds of
different kinds are considered delicacies. Their size varies from that of
a walnut to a grapefruit. The most common truffle is the black variety.
Spore dispersal is accomplished through fungi-eating animals, particularly voles (small rodents), pigs, and flying squirrels. Dogs (mongrels, not
pure breeds) and people can be trained to find truffles. Goats and bears
have also been used.

Where They Come From

Although the traditional gourmet world considers European (especially Italian and French) varieties to be the tastiest, American chefs are embracing domestic fungi, which can be obtained for a fraction of the cost and which are also likely to be fresher. Some American truffles have received poor reviews because they have been harvested before they are ripe; however, many are rated very good with an excellent cost-to-value ratio. Most North American truffles come from Oregon.

Why They Are Prized

In 2007, the world's largest truffle (3.3 pounds) sold at an international auction for $330,000. Truffles are both very aromatic and rare. Difficult to find, very difficult to cultivate, and with a very short growing season, truffles are best when eaten fresh and taste like no other earthly food. Truffles are considered an acquired taste. White truffles, the most treasured, are also the most aromatic and are harvested from September to December in particular regions of Italy and France.

How to Select Fresh Truffles

Although different locales have different seasons, the most flavorful truffles peak in midwinter. Truffles are priced by weight (not size) and categorized according to color—black or white—and season—winter or summer—but within these categories, the truffles are graded. These marks of quality are: super extra, which are best, largest (about size of a grapefruit), and quite rare; extra grade, which are oblong and about the size of ping-pong balls; and first choice, which are lower in grade, smaller in size (berries), more available, and affordable. The size of a truffle does not affect its aroma, flavor, or quality.

What to Do When Fresh Truffles Are Not Available or Are Too Expensive

Flash-frozen truffles, both European and domestic, are available year-round from many different sources. Frozen truffles can retain some of the aroma and most of the taste of the fresh ones. Canned and jarred truffles are sterilized, destroying almost all the aroma and much of the taste. Other types include whole truffles, chopped/sliced truffles, peeled truffles, and brushed truffles (to remove the dirt).

WHAT YOU MAY WANT TO KNOW

❖ Truffles taste best within a few days after being unearthed.

❖ To clean fresh truffles, do not wash until the day of use. Gently rinse with water; brush with a vegetable brush, toothbrush, or nailbrush, then pat lightly with a paper towel.

❖ What to serve with truffles: something bland, with little flavor, such as eggs, rice, potatoes, or pasta. However, they do combine very well with garlic, onions, leeks, scallions, and celery. For recipes with eggs, rice, or potatoes, placing the truffles with them in a closed container for one or two days prior to preparation will infuse them with the truffle aroma, ensuring more flavor!

❖ What to incorporate truffles into: butter, cheese spreads, pates, terrines, and mousses.

❖ How to shave fresh truffles: Use a good-quality truffle slicer. Firmly gripping the slicer, shave a paper-thin slice from any side of the truffle; continue to shave truffle from the same side. Do not turn or flip the truffle, as there is a risk of cracking it, and the remainder will not store as well as it will be more prone to oxidation.

❖ How to preserve truffles: A truffle exposed to humidity will lose its perfume. If keeping in the refrigerator for a few days, wrap tightly in plastic wrap or cover with goose fat, duck fat, or an oil that has no taste. Freezing (for up to six months) preserves most of its aroma. Traditionally, truffles are stored for short periods in jars or trays of rice.

❖ Truffle prices fluctuate daily; adding truffle slices to your restaurant pasta can be very expensive.

WHAT YOU MAY FIND HELPFUL TO KNOW

❖ Truffle accessories: For an elegant presentation, truffles are shaved with a special mandolin called a *taglia tartufo* and are frequently presented on a truffle bell tray. The typical truffle slicer/shaver has a very sharp stainless steel blade that can be adjusted for various thicknesses.

❖ Truffle products: The wonderful flavors of truffles are less expensively found in truffle oils, purees, sea salt, cream, risotto, flour, and dried pastas, pastes, and sauces. Truffle-infused olive oil is the most popular.

❖ Beware: there are many imitation truffle products, especially white truffle oils, which may contain synthetically produced truffle essence.

❖ Truffle etiquette: a maitre d' or chef who shaves a truffle first on one side and then the other may lack knowledge, skill, and/or proper truffle etiquette—and may be compromising your truffle!

❖ Truffles are especially aromatic because they must attract hungry animals—pigs, voles, and flying squirrels, in particular—to spread their spores.

❖ The Italian dessert of an ice cream ball coated with chocolate shavings and nuts is called *tartuffo,* the Italian word for truffle.

❖ Truffles have been called fairy apples, black pearls, diamonds of cookery, the ultimate luxury, gems of poor lands, holy of holies for the gourmet, and black queen, to name a few monikers.

❖ During the appropriate season, you can add a truffle-hunting trip to your European itinerary.

❖ How to grow your own truffles: purchase seedling trees inoculated with truffles; properly prepare the soil with correct alkaline level; irrigate, aerate, and control weeds; and wait for several years before reaping the fruit of your fungi. Good Luck!

WHAT NOT TO DO

❖ Peel truffles, as the peel and body together create the full truffle experience.

❖ Cook with real truffle-infused olive oil, as it is quite delicate and will lose its aroma.

❖ Put truffles into a grinder or food mill. If crushing, use a fork.

❖ Touch the truffle when purchasing. According to truffle etiquette, you may only look and smell.

Anyone who does not declare himself ready to leave heaven or hell for such a treat is not worthy to be born again.

–Maurice Goudeket

Finger Bowls

Don't drink from your finger bowl—it contains only
water.

–Anonymous

The finger bowl is a small glass bowl of cool or lukewarm water used for rinsing the fingers at the table. It is considered by some to be a pretentious or outmoded ritual as well as the most confusing part of a formal dinner. Any food that can be eaten with the fingers will leave a slight residue and odor, and finger bowls can be a practical addition to a messy meal and sticky digits. Although you may see only one or two finger bowls in your lifetime, those occasions will most likely be important events in your professional or personal life. Using one properly will impress your host and other guests.

WHAT YOU NEED TO KNOW

❖ How to recognize a finger bowl when you see it: although finger bowls may be used at any time during a meal, they are usually passed at the close of a meal before the dessert course. The bowl is traditionally presented on a dessert plate with a doily beneath.

❖ If you find a lemon slice, flower, or scented leaf floating in your bowl, do not squeeze it or take it out—or eat it.

❖ One hand at a time, dip only the tips of your fingers into the finger bowl.

❖ To dry: quickly and discreetly place your fingertips on your napkin, which is held low in your lap and below table level.

❖ After you have cleaned and dried your fingers, move the doily and the bowl together to the top left corner of your place setting (where your bread plate was originally placed), so that the plate will be ready for the dessert course.

WHAT YOU MAY WANT TO KNOW

❖ If the bowl is served with a fork and/or spoon, do not use them with the finger bowl. They are dessert utensils. Before using the finger bowl, place the fork to the left and the spoon to the right of your dessert plate.

❖ Occasionally, a palate cleanser, such as a fruit sorbet, is presented after the finger bowl and prior to the actual dessert or cheese course.

WHAT YOU MAY FIND HELPFUL TO KNOW

❖ Always use both hands to lift the bowl.

❖ The fingerbowl is sometimes used after or during a fruit course, when the fruit is served as part of a breakfast or brunch.

- ❖ The finger bowl may be accompanied by a fresh napkin, which is later removed by the server. The entire finger bowl ritual should be completed effortlessly and unobtrusively.

- ❖ The fingerbowl can be a lovely addition to a formal meal. For example, the leaves or flowers used can coordinate with the theme or centerpiece.

WHAT NOT TO DO

- ❖ Drink from the fingerbowl.

- ❖ Place or dip your napkin into the bowl.

- ❖ Shake water from your fingers.

- ❖ Splash, swish, or swirl.

- ❖ Place anything into the water except your fingertips.

- ❖ Use the finger bowl for cleaning your face or your entire hand.

- ❖ Wipe your fingers on the doily beneath the bowl.

- ❖ Share fingerbowls.

- ❖ Leave the bowl on plate when finished.

How To Eat

HOW TO EAT ARTICHOKES

These things are just plain annoying. After all the trouble
you go to, you get about as much actual "food" out of
eating an artichoke as you would from licking thirty or
forty postage stamps. Have the shrimp cocktail instead.

—Miss Piggy

Artichokes are edible perennial herbs most often used as vegetables. The most common and most difficult variety to eat, the globe artichoke, has an edible core called the heart—a clump of closely packed, tender, unformed leaves. It comes in two sizes—regular and baby. Some baby artichokes are completely edible. Do not confuse the globe with artichokes that have edible roots—the Jerusalem and the Chinese. The edible part of a Jerusalem artichoke (also known as a sunchoke) is its tuber, which can be grated raw for use in salads or incorporated into many recipes from brisket and pickles to soups and latkes. The less familiar Chinese artichoke is an herb cultivated for its crisp sweet tubers that can be eaten raw or boiled, steamed, or baked. Whole globe artichokes may be steamed or boiled and may be served hot or cold, plain or stuffed.

❖ Beginning at the bottom of the artichoke, pull off the large outer petals, one at a time. The leaves of the well-cooked artichoke will almost fall off of the stem.

❖ Holding the top of a leaf as if it were a potato chip, dip the light fleshy end (which was attached to the stem) into the butter or dipping sauce. Typical sauces are hot butter, garlic-flavored mayonnaise, oil and vinegar, and various types of salad dressings. Lemon slices are also a suitable accompaniment.

❖ Still gripping the top of the leaf, place it into your mouth, preferably dip side down, and pull through teeth to remove the soft meat at the bottom of the leaf. Do NOT eat the entire leaf.

❖ Discard the leaf on your artichoke plate or another plate or dish that your host has provided.

❖ Continue until all leaves have been removed and you reach the middle.

❖ In the middle, you will find an inedible, fuzzy "choke" covering the artichoke heart. With a spoon or knife, scrape it out and discard (in the same place as the petals), uncovering the bottom, which is the delicious and coveted heart.

❖ Using a knife and fork, cut the heart into pieces, dip into the sauce, and eat.

❖ After removing any stringy or hard parts, you can also eat the stem.

A stuffed artichoke will not be dipped and may be messier to eat. Common stuffings, which are spooned onto the leaves, include bread crumbs, various cheeses, mashed hard-boiled eggs—even crab meat.

Artichokes are frequently presented on artichoke plates—a plate with a recess in the middle for the artichoke as well as an indentation on the side for a dipping sauce. Discarded leaves are placed around the perimeter of the plate. Otherwise, your host will provide additional bowls.

> At least you'll never be a vegetable—even artichokes have hearts.
>
> —From the film *Amelie*

HOW TO EAT CRUSTACEANS:
LOBSTER, CRAB, CRAYFISH, AND SHRIMP

LOBSTER

A truly destitute man is not one without riches but the
poor wretch who has never partaken of lobster.

–Anonymous

This marine crustacean with large pincers is delightfully delicious but notoriously difficult to eat. Its hard shell, many different anatomical parts, small meat morsels, and resultant messiness are all challenging for the novice. If you are selecting your own lobster, you may need to choose whether you prefer a soft-shell or a hard-shell lobster. The shells of soft-shell, or new-shell, lobsters are easy to break apart. The meat is quite sweet. However, they do not transport very well in their post-molt condition. The more common hard-shells contain firmer meat, but it is more difficult to extract. Lobster meat spoils very quickly, so lobster is cooked while it still alive. If you are served a lobster with a flat, uncurled tail, do not eat it: it was dead when it was cooked, so you will not know how fresh it is!

Lobster tails vary in size, color, and taste. They include African, Australian, New Zealand, Maine, and Brazilian.

How to Eat a Whole Lobster

❖ To help you remove the warm or chilled meat from a cooked whole lobster, you will be given a lobster cracker, a pick, or small lobster/cocktail fork and, sometimes, a bib. Lobster shears or sea scissors can also be helpful. There are no set rules for the order in which you disassemble or eat a lobster. However, before eating, you may *wish to take your lobster apart. First, grasp the lobster by its back and gently twist the legs (small claws) off the lobster and place them on the side of the plate. Next, tear or twist off the claws at the first joint. Separate the tail piece from the body by arching the back until it cracks and then twist. Break the flippers from the tail piece.*

❖ Of course, this entire process can be avoided if you order or are served stuffed lobster or lobster thermidor, a rich, complex, and delicious French dish that combines cooked lobster meat with cream, eggs, butter, and Cognac, sherry, or vermouth—all stuffed into a lobster shell and usually topped with a cheese sauce

How to Eat Tail Meat

❖ Insert your fork, pick, or sometimes your finger where the flippers broke off and push the tail meat out intact through the larger opening. Then, peel off the top of the tail to reveal the digestive tract, which should be removed before eating the remainder of the tail meat.

How to Eat Claw Meat

❖ Crack each claw and remove the meat with a fork or pick.

How to Eat Leg Meat

❖ After breaking the legs at their joints, you can remove little bits of meat with your pick or lobster fork. As in the famous film scene of Tom Jones and his paramour snapping and juicily sucking lobster legs, in less formal and more exuberantly hungry company, it is acceptable to bite and suck the ends of the legs to enjoy the final morsels and juice.

❖ Dip the warm meat into accompanying clarified butter or lemon butter or dip cold meat into mayonnaise.

Lobster Lore

❖ Lobster lovers also eat the green and red "stuff." The green tomalley is the lobster's digestive system; the red coral, considered a delicacy by many, is the unfertilized egg of the female.

❖ Lobster meat contains omega-3 fatty acids and has fewer calories than equivalent amounts of chicken or steak.

❖ Lobsters and crabs are safe to eat when there is a "shellfish ban" because they do not filter plankton from seawater.

CRAB

You cannot teach a crab to walk straight.

–Aristophanes

There are almost five thousand different species of crabs worldwide. They all have ten legs, walk sideways, have eyes that jut out on stalks, and have a protective crust-like shell. They are delicious and succulent but are definitely not fast food. Steamed crabs are usually served with shell crackers or wooden mallets for breaking open the shells, and with picks, small forks, or crab forks (which have a round scoop on one end and a small fork on the other) for removing the meat. As with lobster, crab can be served with a wide variety of sauces.

The edible crabs most frequently eaten in the United States are the king, blue, snow, Dungeness, and soft-shell. The brown crab and spider crab are sometimes imported but are mainly consumed in European countries. Horseshoe crabs are seldom eaten, although their roe is used in cooking, and hermit crabs can make fascinating, low-maintenance family pets.

How to Eat Crabs with Hard Shells

❖ Twist off the claws and pinchers. Crack the shell with a cracker or mallet. Use your hands to pull the shell open and use the fork to pull out the meat. Eat as is or dip into the sauce. Use the cracker to split the larger legs—especially king and snow crab legs—and then pull out the meat with a fork or suck the meat out.

❖ Do not eat the white, crescent-shaped lungs. Remove them to find more crabmeat underneath.

❖ Crab gourmands enjoy eating the reddish orange "stuff", the roe of the female crab. It is also used to flavor other popular dishes, such as South Carolina's famous she-crab soup.

How to Eat Soft-Shell Crab

❖ Usually served fried, soft-shell crab requires no special implements, and the crab is eaten whole—shell and all!

❖ Frequently pan-fried with almonds, it can be eaten with any seafood condiment or sauce. Use a knife and fork to cut the crab down the middle and then into bite-size portions. You can eat the legs entirely, but some suck out the crabmeat and leave the inedible parts on their plates. It is also popularly served as a sandwich.

❖ Soft-shell crabs are crabs that have just molted their exoskeleton and are soft for a brief period before their new shell hardens. The soft-shell crab season is April to October on the Gulf Coast. The season is shorter on the East Coast—the water temperature must be above 50 degrees.

Crayfish: a small crustacean very much resembling the lobster, but less indigestible.

–Ambrose Bierce

Known also as crawfish and crawdads, crayfish are fresh-water crustaceans that resemble small lobsters. In Louisiana, crayfish are a favorite local delicacy, but they are also popular in restaurants and seafood stores throughout the United States. Fortunately, most crayfish boils take place out of doors because eating boiled crayfish for the first time can be both intimidating and messy.

How to Eat Crayfish

❖ Remove the head by twisting it from the tail. Holding the very end of the tail with one hand, pull the tail meat out with the other. Some devotees suck the head before discarding it.

SHRIMP

Shrimp is the fruit of the sea. You can barbecue it, bake it, boil it, broil it, sauté it. There's, um, shrimp kebabs, shrimp Creole, shrimp gumbo, pan fried, deep fried, stir-fried. There's pineapple shrimp and lemon shrimp, pepper shrimp, shrimp soup, shrimp stew, shrimp salad, shrimp and potatoes, shrimp burger, shrimp sandwich. That's about it.

–Forrest Gump

Depending on how they are served, shrimp can be very easy to eat or can take a bit of work to peel. They are usually served with a sauce, such as cocktail, remoulade, or Louis.

As Hors D'oeuvres

❖ These shrimp are usually served with tails on and are eaten with the fingers. Pick it up by the tail and dip into the sauce—no double dipping. Hosts usually provide extra bowls for tails; otherwise leave them on your plate. After eating, do not place your tails directly onto the server's tray.

In Shrimp Cocktail

❖ Smaller shrimp are usually peeled and deveined, requiring only that you spear them with your cocktail fork, dip into the sauce, and pop into your mouth. Shrimp too large to eat in one bite should be cut on the plate.

❖ Sometimes larger shrimp are peeled and deveined but still have their tails. These can be eaten by holding onto the tail unless they are really large, in which case they should be placed onto dish to cut with knife and fork.

In Main Courses

❖ Most shrimp served as a main course can be eaten with a knife and fork. However, shrimp in some dishes, such as garlic prawns, are unpeeled.

❖ To peel a shrimp, turn the shrimp on its back. Place your thumbs in the middle near the top of the shrimp and pull the shell apart; the shell usually comes off in one piece. Keep the tail intact if you wish to use it as a handle. Remove the vein along the top (spine) of the shrimp if it has not already been removed.

❖ Fantail shrimp, which are battered and crisply fried, are usually eaten while holding the tail, rather than with a knife and fork.

HOW TO EAT BONE MARROW

I went to the woods because I wanted to live deliberately. I wanted to suck out all the marrow of life.

–Henry David Thoreau

Animal bone marrow is the fatty vascular tissue that fills most bone cavities. Highly caloric, nutrient dense, and truly delicious, most marrow that is served comes from mature cows but also from other large mammals, including pigs, calves, and oxen. Most of us have enjoyed soups and stocks that have been seasoned with bones and their marrow, and many have feasted on the meat and marrow of crosscut veal shank (the Italian favorite osso buco, meaning "bone with a hole"), but few of us have enjoyed our marrow "straight up."

How to Prepare and Serve

❖ Roasting the bones upright is the most common preparation, and the diner's most common predicament is how to extricate the marrow from the inside of the bone. A narrow spoon or fork can be used to scrape out the marrow, but most restaurants provide a dedicated marrow spoon or scoop. Made of metal, both spoon and scoop have long narrow handles and gulleys. The spoons were widely used during the reign of Queen Anne; however, by the end of the eighteenth century, marrow spoons were rapidly being superseded by marrow scoops, which have a scoop on each end, one roughly twice the length of the other. Restaurants and hosts may use silver, silver-plate, or stainless-steel utensils. Most antique silver marrow spoons and scoops have become collector's items, especially those with certain hallmarks.

❖ Traditionally, roasted marrow is served with a side of sea salt, some fresh parsley, and crisp toast or bread to slather it on. However, chefs also pair it with anchovies, watercress, shallot, confit, small green salad, chopped egg, salsa verde—and even orange–olive marmalade.

❖ And, yes, although sucking or gnawing on rich, creamy, marrow bones may help you to savor every last bit, please do it in private—definitely not on a first date.

Oh literature, oh the glorious Art, how it preys upon the marrow in our bones. It scoops the stuffing out of us and chucks us aside. Alas!

–D. H. Lawrence

HOW TO EAT A POMEGRANATE

In every pomegranate, a decayed pip is to be found.

–Latin proverb

omegranates have been symbols of prosperity and abundance in many civilizations, and they feature prominently in their art and religious and secular literature. Pliny wrote about how to preserve pomegranates, the Bible makes many references to pomegranates, Homer mentions them in *The Odyssey*, and Shakespeare describes picking kernels out of pomegranates in *All's Well That Ends Well*. Sometimes referred to as a Chinese apple, many scholars believe that the forbidden fruit that Eve found irresistible in the Garden of Eden was actually a pomegranate, not an apple.

Native to Iran, the reddish, orange-sized fruit and its juice have become popular for its flavorful taste as well as its many health benefits. The thick rind contains waxy white chambers that hold many seeds, or arils, covered with red, juicy pulp. Difficult to de-seed and messy to eat, they were obviously intended for our slow enjoyment. As pomegranates do not ripen after they are picked and dry out quickly while stored, the ripest, freshest pomegranates can be found at farmers' markets or stores that receive deliveries directly from farmers. The juice is also the basis of grenadine syrup, used in flavorings and liqueurs.

There is no "right" way to get at the juicy insides of a pomegranate. As each fruit can contain between two hundred and two thousand seeds, any method can seem time-consuming. To get at those sweet, juicy seeds with a minimum of mess and effort, try this:

❖ Rinse in water. Cut off the crown (stem end) and discard.

❖ Score the rind with a large X at least halfway down fruit, being careful not to cut all the way through.

❖ Place the pomegranate in a bowl of water and allow to soak for five to ten minutes.

❖ Break sections of the fruit open in the bowl.

❖ While the fruit is submerged, use your fingers to carefully brush seeds from the membrane. The seeds will sink to the bottom, and the membrane will float. Holding the fruit side down in the water will keep seeds from squirting you. A strainer can be useful with this process.

❖ Discard the rind, drain, and enjoy.

❖ The small seeds within the red pulp are meant to be eaten. If you do not care for them, do not spit them out when in the company of others. Simply do not eat fresh pomegranate.

HOW TO EAT ESCARGOT
IN THE SHELL

It's all about how we phrase things: people eat escargot, not snails.

Considered a delicacy, escargot is a dish of cooked land snails, usually served as an appetizer. Especially popular in France and in French restaurants worldwide, the snails are removed from their shells, purged, and gutted and then prepared with garlic, butter, and parsley. Once back in their shells, they are usually placed on escargot dishes and eaten with special implements. Escargots are rich in protein, low in fat (without the butter sauce), and high in water content (about 80 percent).

How to Eat Escargot

❖ Escargot is usually presented on china dishes or metal trays with depressions for six or twelve snails. Sometimes there is a cavity to hold extra butter sauce in the middle, or it is served on the side. Your server will bring special escargot tongs for holding the shell and slender, two-pronged escargot forks for extracting the meat.

❖ Grip the shell with the tongs or hold it with a napkin-covered hand. With the other hand, use the fork to retrieve the escargot. Place the empty shell back into its cavity. Dip the escargot into butter sauce and enjoy.

❖ The French, and some other cultures, also serve small sea snails (periwinkles), which have been boiled in the shell. Much tinier and tastier than land snails, they come with small picks or thin wooden skewers for picking out them out of the shell.

HOW TO EAT (AND ORDER) SUSHI AND SASHIMI

The Japanese characters for sushi translate to "delicious fish."

Described as edible art, sushi is rice, cooked, vinegared, and cooled (*shari*), then combined with other ingredients. It is wrapped with a sheet of pressed seaweed (*nori*), usually black but also in light colors. Good sushi possesses a harmonious balance of taste and texture. Sashimi is very fresh raw fish, sliced and served by itself without rice or seaweed.

Soy sauce (*shoyu*), wasabi (*pungent Japanese horseradish*), and sweet pickled ginger root (*gari*) are usually served with sushi and sashimi. Sashimi is frequently placed on top of shiso leaves, a popular Japanese savory herb. Both are accompanied by green tea.

Because Japanese dining has many traditions, rules, and nuances, learning certain behaviors will certainly make your dining experience more pleasant

Types of Sushi

❖ There are two main types—*nigiri* and *maki*. *Nigiri-zushi* is *shari* shaped into bite-sized pieces topped with raw seafood and often wrapped with strips of *nori*. *Maki-zushi* is strips of vegetables and/or fish wrapped with *shari* and *nori,* that is fashioned into a roll and sliced into round bite-size pieces.

❖ Handroll sushi, or *temaki-zushi,* is a small square of *nori* wrapped around fish and/or vegetables and shaped into a cone. It is also popular and can be easily eaten with the hands.

- The fish used for sushi is usually raw but can also be pickled or cooked. Crab, shrimp, octopus, and eel (often marinated first) are all cooked before being used to make sushi.

- The increasing popularity of sushi has resulted in the creation of many varieties to suit the Western palate. These include the ubiquitous California roll as well as Alaska rolls, Seattle rolls, mango rolls, rainbow rolls, and spider rolls (containing soft-shell crab). The inside-out roll has rice on the outside as well as the inside.

Etiquette for Eating Sushi

- Eat *nigiri* and *maki-zushi* in one bite.

- You may use either chopsticks or fingers to dip sushi into soy sauce—fish side down. The rice has been carefully seasoned with vinegar, so the soy sauce would ruin the balance of the taste of the rice. Also, the first taste of the fish (and soy sauce) is considered better than that of the rice.

- *Gunkan,* sushi that is topped with materials such as salmon roe, flying fish roe, sea urchin, or certain flavorings, would fall apart if turned over and require another approach: dip your *gari* into the soy sauce and use it to transfer the liquid to the surface of the *gunkan.*

- Always eat sushi as soon as possible after it is served, particularly in sushi restaurants. It is customary to eat sashimi before eating sushi.

Sushi Bar Etiquette

- You will first be served a cup of hot green tea and given a small damp towel (*oshibori*) for wiping your hands.

- You can look at the displays in front of you and watch the chef preparing various dishes to help you determine your order.

- If seated at a sushi bar, ask the sushi chef (*itamae*) only for sushi. All items other than sushi and sashimi, such as drinks and soup, are handled by the server.

- Although there is no rule in placing orders, it is generally recommended to start with the lighter taste and progress to heavier/more fatty sushi, occasionally refreshing your palate with *gari*.

- Foreigners' tendency to request extra wasabi is considered gauche. Excessive wasabi disguises the other tastes and exposes the novice.

- Rather than order from the menu, you may ask the chef to serve you his recommendations because he knows what is best that day and in which order to serve them. He may ask you if there are any fish you particularly like or dislike.

- Leave a tip for the *itamae* in the tip jar (Western cultures) because the chef will not touch the money.

- Thank the *itamae*.

WHAT NOT TO DO

- Rub your chopsticks together (unless they are very cheap with obvious splinters or you are trying to start a fire).

- Suck on your chopsticks.

- Spear food with your chopstick(s).

❖ Peel fish off the rice in order to dip it in soy cause and then put it back on the rice.

❖ Ask the *itamae* if something is fresh.

❖ Leave food on your plate.

❖ Mix wasabi into your soy sauce when eating *nigiri* or *maki-zushi*.

❖ Eat sashimi with your hands.

❖ Put *gari* on your wrapped sushi. Instead, eat it between sushi to cleanse your palate, preparing your taste buds for the next flavor.

❖ Pick up a piece of food from another person's plate with the end of the chopsticks you put in your mouth.

❖ Ask for a soup spoon if you are not given one. You are expected to pick up the bowl to drink your soup.

❖ Pass food to another person using chopsticks (an action that is similar to the passing of a deceased person's bones at a Japanese funeral). Rather, use a plate to pass food.

❖ Leave your chopsticks sticking into your rice bowl or other dish (like incense). Place them on a chopstick rest.

HOW TO EAT FROG LEGS

Better to eat than to kiss.

–A princess

A delicacy in many parts of the world, farm-raised frog legs have a subtle flavor somewhere between chicken and fish. They resemble small, skinny, long poultry legs. Many cuisines—Asian, South American, and French—grill, broil, fry, or boil the legs, incorporating their various herbs and spices. Typical French grenouilles are coated with flour, pan-fried, or grilled and served with a lemon and/or garlic butter.

How to Eat Frog Legs

❖ Pick up the legs with your hand, as you would small pieces of fried chicken. Disjoint large legs with a knife and fork before eating. Always hold the leg with one hand, not two.

Alert

❖ You may observe that some French prepare and eat the entire headless frog body, gutted and served with garlic butter, herbs de Provence, and parsley. These are a different, much smaller species, about three inches in total size. You will also see dried frogs being sold in Asian markets.

HOW TO EAT SPAGHETTI
(LIKE AN ITALIAN)

A piece of spaghetti or a military unit can only be led from the front end.

–General George S. Patton

It is true that some restaurants and hosts provide their pasta-eating guests with a knife, fork, and large spoon. However, spaghetti and other forms of long thin pasta (usually ten to twelve inches in length) are correctly eaten with only a fork. The pasta is usually served in a bowl (sometimes a plate) with the majority of the sauce in the center. If your place setting includes a large spoon, it may be used to spoon your sauce on top and, with the fork, to help toss the sauce and cheese with the pasta. If your meal includes a bib, you are free to use it.

The more al dente (the preferred consistency of firm but not hard) the pasta is cooked, the more difficult it will be for the novice to eat: overcooked pasta fits more neatly and easily around the fork.

How to Eat Pasta with a Fork

❖ Place your fork vertically in the center of your plate. Holding it upright, twirl the fork, rolling a few strands of spaghetti around the tines.

❖ Raise your fork to determine the size of the bundle and the length of any trailing strands. If the pasta looks too large or too long to eat in one bite, drop it down and pick up a smaller bunch. Have a napkin ready to use. Practice at home.

How to Eat Pasta with a Spoon

❖ Hold your spoon in your non-dominant hand. Spear a few strands of spaghetti with your fork. Place the tips into the bowl of the spoon and twirl the fork, wrapping the spaghetti around itself. Put a reasonably sized bite into your mouth. The spoon method is simpler and is considered appropriate for children and for amateurs.

WHAT NOT TO DO

❖ Use the bread to wipe up the last bits of sauce on your plate at a formal dinner. This is called *fare la scarpetta*, meaning "to do the little shoe." (Although it is usually on the table, purists do not serve or eat bread with pasta.)

❖ Use a knife and/or fork to cut threads of pasta.

❖ Slurp.

❖ Vigorously shake your fork to drop some strands.

❖ Use a napkin as a bib.

Everything you see I owe to spaghetti.

–Sophia Loren

HOW TO EAT SOUP

Good manners: the noise you don't make when you are eating soup.

–Bennett Cerf, humorist, publisher

Every detail of the formal meal, including even how you eat your soup, contributes to your overall image—professional and personal. A liquid food made by boiling or simmering meat, fish, fruit, and/or vegetables with added flavorful ingredients, soup may be clear or may contain small or large morsels of meat, fish, vegetables, or other food. Soups may be served either hot or cold, although some might consider "cold soup" an oxymoron.

Soup bowls are served with their own saucer or underplate or are placed on the service plate/charger. The texture, temperature, and amount of the soup served determine both the size and shape of the bowl. Because they retain heat well, thick, chunky soups can be served in wide, shallow bowls, while pureed soups stay warm in deep bowls or narrow cups. Bouillon and consommé are served in small, two-handled cups. Covered soup bowls are used for soup that needs to be kept hot. The most informal soup bowl is the plain coupe bowl. The ovenproof lug soup bowl is often used for French onion soup.

Soupspoons are usually larger than teaspoons with deeper bowls. The round soupspoon is usually used with cream soups; the more versatile oval spoon (sometimes a dessert spoon) can be used for most other soups. Some silver patterns use size to differentiate between bouillon, cream, and gumbo spoons.

How to Eat Properly

❖ Insert the spoon into your soup sideways near the edge of bowl.

❖ Fill it only three-quarters full and draw it away from you toward the back of the bowl.

❖ Sip from the side of the spoon. You may tip the soup bowl away from you to retrieve the last spoonful. When you are finished, leave the spoon on the soup plate. If the soup was served in a cup, place the spoon on the saucer or underplate.

Special Soup Manners

❖ When eating traditional French onion soup, first break through the melted cheese and crouton topping and twirl piece of cheese onto your spoon. Press the edge of the spoon against the bowl to cut off the cheese strand and eat the cheese and bread. Continue eating the soup and topping, biting off dangling cheese strands so that they fall into the bowl of your spoon.

❖ When eating bouillon or consommé, you may use either the small spoon or drink (sip) from the cup using either one or two hands. Do not do both. If your soup comes with a lid, remove it to the side of your underplate and then replace it before the table is cleared.

Cracker Manners

❖ Place oyster crackers onto your underplate so that you can add them to your soup a few at a time. Place larger crackers, such as saltines, on your bread plate and eat with fingers or crumble over soup. Croutons, which are passed in a serving dish, may be sprinkled directly onto your soup with the small serving spoon provided.

Garnish Manners

❖ Use a serving spoon or your clean soupspoon to sprinkle toppings directly onto your soup. Place the serving spoon back on the garnish's underplate. Always garnish soups *before* beginning to eat.

WHAT NOT TO DO

❖ Blow on hot soup.

❖ Slurp.

❖ Overfill your soupspoon.

❖ Place the entire bowl of the spoon into your mouth.

❖ Eat your bread with one hand while holding your soup-spoon in the other.

❖ Pick up your soup bowl to drink the last drops.

❖ Place your used spoon directly on the tablecloth.

❖ Confuse bouillon (broth) with the hearty Haitian meat-and-vegetable soup of the same name.

Soup is cuisine's kindest course. It breathes reassurance;
it steams consolation; after a weary day, it promotes
sociability, as the five o'clock cup of tea or the cocktail
hour.

–Louis P. De Gouy, *The Soup Book*

HOW TO EAT BOUILLABAISSE

This Bouillabaisse a noble dish is—
A sort of soup or broth or brew,
Or hotchpotch of all sorts of fishes,
That Greenwich never could outdo;
Green herbs, red peppers, mussels, saffron.
Soles, onions, garlic, roach, and dace;
All these you eat at Terre's tavern,
In that one dish of Bouillabaisse.

–William Makepeace Thackeray, "Ballad of Bouillabaisse"

T*o properly eat bouillabaisse, a well-known French dish, you must know what it is and how it is served. This classic Provencal seafood stew is a highly seasoned broth containing several varieties of fish and shellfish and vegetables. Traditional ingredients include tomatoes, olive oil, leeks, garlic, Pernod, parsley, white wine, fennel, orange peel, and saffron, a signature ingredient. An authentic bouillabaisse includes at least three types of Mediterranean seafood. However, more modern versions are made with local seafood, such as snapper, cod, octopus, and shrimp.*

Often preceded by a simple green salad and served in two parts with various accompaniments, bouillabaisse is a meal in itself. The first part of the serving is a large bowl of flavorful golden brown broth. The second part is a shallow dish filled with fish and shellfish spread over a bed of sliced potatoes and broth. Complements include a small bowl or boat of mustard sauce, Parmesan cheese, and toasted bread. An orange-red mayonnaise-like sauce called rouille (similar to aioli), made of olive oil, garlic, saffron, chili peppers, saffron, capsicum, and onion accompanies the broth.

How to Eat Bouillabaisse

❖ You will use the soupspoon for the broth but will need to know which implements—shellfish crackers, seafood fork, or knife—are used for the types of seafood served (i.e., crab, mussels, lobster, scallops, shrimp, etc.).

❖ The mustard sauce and/or cheese are spread on the bread or toast, and then the bread is placed in the soup until it becomes nicely soggy so that it can be eaten with a spoon.

❖ The distinctively flavored *rouille* is spread on the toast, which can be placed in the broth or eaten separately.

❖ Many modern restaurants now serve a first course of the broth, bread, cheese, mustard sauce, and *rouille*, leaving the actual fish and seafood as the second course. There will be an empty bowl for your discarded shells and bones.

PART TWO

BEFORE AND
AFTER DINNER

SERVING BEVERAGES

When offering beverages to your guests, always be sure that you provide nonalcoholic alternatives for cocktails, aperitifs, wines, and after-dinner drinks. Offer cocktail napkins for drinks not served at the dinner table. If you are serving beverages before the meal, anywhere from thirty minutes to an hour is an acceptable time period. When hosting or greeting, hold your drink glass in your left hand so that the next person you greet will not receive a cold, wet reception.

APERITIFS

Drinking a small amount of alcohol before a meal dates back to the ancient Egyptians! Intended to stimulate the appetite, the aperitif (meaning "to open") is an alcoholic beverage that is served before the meal. The many choices include champagne, sherry, vermouth, Campari, Lillet, Dubonnet, ouzo, or dry white wine. Although usually served unmixed, there are some popular aperitif cocktails. Usually served elsewhere, the unfinished aperitif is not taken to the dinner table.

BRANDIES, LIQUEURS,
AND CORDIALS

BRANDY

Meaning *"burnt wine,"* brandy is a spirit that is produced by distilling wine (70 to 120 US proof) from fermented fruits, usually grapes. Some brandies, such as Cognac and Armagnac, are named for the regions from which they originate. Distilled from fruits other than grapes, fruit brandies are produced in many countries and come in different varieties: apple, pear, apricot, cherry, and blackberry are frequently distilled for brandy. Pomace brandy is produced from fermentation and distillation of grape skins, seeds, and stems. Both the European Union and the United States have specific regulatory requirements regarding the labeling of products identified as brandy. A minimum of six months of aging in oak is required by the European Union; and in the United States, any brandy that has not been aged in oak for at least two years must be labeled "immature."

Brandies Are Categorized by Age

* ❖ AC: Aged a minimum of two years.

* ❖ VS (Very Special): Aged at least three years.

* ❖ VSOP (Very Special Old Pale): Aged at least fifty-five years.

* ❖ XO (Extra Old): Aged at least six years.

* ❖ Vintage: Stamped with the date it was originally stored.

* ❖ Hors D'age: Aged in the barrel at least ten years.

To Serve

❖ Brandy can be served neat, on the rocks, or added to other beverages to make brandy cocktails or special hot drinks. When served as an after-dinner drink, brandy is usually savored neat in a bowl-shaped snifter intended to show its color and release the aroma. You may ask or be asked if you wish to have your glass heated before pouring. If you are hosting, slowly pour a small amount of brandy into the guest's snifter, swirling it gently into the glass.

To Drink

❖ Hold the snifter in your cupped palm to warm the brandy, releasing the aromas and making the taste more pungent. You may hold it to the light to appreciate its color. Swirl the glass while inhaling and enjoying its distinctive aroma. Then sip slowly and savor on the tongue.

❖ Thoroughly cleaning and air-drying the snifter will eliminate any tastes that might interfere with that of the brandy.

WHAT NOT TO DO

❖ Overheat the brandy, as excessive heat may cause the alcohol vapor to become too strong.

LIQUEURS AND CORDIALS

Sweet and syrupy, liqueurs and cordials are usually served with dessert at the table or as an after-dinner drink in another room or area. Frequently accompanied by coffee or demitasse, liqueurs are poured into small (1 or 1 ½ ounces) glasses, usually with a stemmed base. They are also combined with various mixes to make a cocktail or combined with coffee. Layered drinks are made by floating different colored liqueurs in separate layers, *creating a striped or rainbow effect.*

A sweetened, flavor-infused alcoholic beverage made from distilled alcohol, a liqueur acquires its flavor from fruit, nuts, flowers, herbs, honey, wood, or chocolate. They are usually not aged very long but may "rest" while the flavors "marry" into a harmonious blend. Crème liqueurs, which have dairy cream added, usually have one primary flavor, such a crème de menthe, which has a mint flavor.

Generics are liqueurs of a particular type that can be produced by any company. Proprietaries are trademarked liqueurs with unique brand names and have their own specific formulas.

The terms bitters (made with herbs and botanicals, with a bitter flavor), schnapps (made from fermented fruit, usually produced in Germany or Austria), and anise (made by distilling anise and other botanicals) encompass a wide variety of flavored spirits.

If served in conjunction with espresso or Turkish coffee, do not also serve milk or cream for the coffee.

SCOTCH

Originally made from malt barley and known as aqua vitae, or "water of life, " as early as the fifteenth century, Scotch whisky (Scotch) was the remedy of choice for many different ailments. In the late eighteenth century, commercial companies began to also distill wheat, maize, and rye to make Scotch. By law, the whisky, whether made of malt (100 percent barley) or grain, must be aged in oak barrels or casks for at least three years, and Scotch distilled from grain must include at least a fraction of malted barley. Barley is malted by soaking it in water until it begins to sprout. Then it is exposed to hot air to stop the germination. Most Scotch is five years or older, although single malt is commonly bottled at ages from ten to twenty-one years. A bottle of "guaranteed-age" whisky has an age statement that includes the age of the youngest whisky contained in the mix. Scotch comes in many flavors and colors—some whisky lovers group the flavors by region.

There are five categories of Scotch whisky: single grain (single distillery), single malt (single distillery), blended grain, blended or vatted malt, and blended (mixture of malt barley and other grains).

Drinking Scotch

❖ Single malt Scotch is generally considered to be the most elite and cosmopolitan choice. Scotch lovers judge their Scotch by color, aroma, flavors, consistency, and the "finish"—the last taste of the malt on the back of the tongue.

❖ Whether for cocktails or after dinner, Scotch can be served with ice, spring water, various mixers, or neat. Serious Scotch drinkers prefer their drink without ice, water, or any mixes.

❖ Fine malt whisky, not meant to be an icy cold drink, is enhanced by the way in which it is served: at room temperature; in a clear glass container (tumbler or snifter), which shows the malt's color and retains its aroma; neat; or by adding a drop or two of water to a full-bodied/cask strength malt to enhance its ability to bring out its flavors and aromas.

❖ When served at the end of a meal as an after-dinner aperitif or later as a nightcap, malt Scotch is frequently offered with a cigar.

❖ Store malt whisky at room temperature as chill can dilute and dull both taste and texture.

WHAT NOT TO DO

❖ Serve Scotch with tap water, as it may contain chlorine and other additives that will distort the taste and aroma

❖ Spell Scotch whisky with an *e*.

WINES

Differences between wines range from very subtle to dramatic, and selecting a wine that complements your course or meal can be both an art and a science. If you are not familiar with the world of wine, asking the expert in your local wine shop for advice or consulting with your sommelier can take the guesswork out of selecting wines as well as the surprise out of the prices.

Now that you have chosen the perfect wines for a dinner party, in a restaurant, at a banquet, or for your own indulgence, the proper opening, tasting, and serving will greatly enhance enjoyment. The menu usually determines the wine; however, if in doubt about enjoying multiple wines, serve white before red, young before old, dry before sweet, and save the best wine until last.

To Chill or Not to Chill

❖ The temperature at which wine is served unquestionably affects its taste and aroma. The general rule of thumb is that white wine should be served chilled, and red wine is served at room temperature. However, the lighter, more refreshing white wines, such as Sauvignon Blanc and Pinot Grigio, should be served at a refrigerator temperature of 35 to 40 degrees Fahrenheit, while the more full-bodied, high-quality white wines taste best at "cellar temperature," or 55 degrees.

❖ Chill wine by placing in the refrigerator for about an hour and a half before serving, allowing it to warm slightly prior to serving.

❖ If the wine needs to be chilled more quickly, place in a container of iced water: It is more effective than placing wine in a bucket of ice.

❖ The "room temperature" of red wines does not mean 75 degrees but refers to European rooms before modern heating. Thus, about 62 to 65 degrees—cool but warmer than "cellar temperature"—is appropriate for serving most red wines.

How to Open

❖ Most wines are sealed with a natural or synthetic cork that is covered with a foil metal cap. Using a sharp knife, foil cutter, or the cutter on the corkscrew, first cut off the top part of the cap.

❖ Although the lever and the butterfly are the most common types of corkscrews, there are many other devices, including electric and air pump, all of which remove corks. Most have a screw-like piece, which is carefully screwed into the cork and then pulled.

❖ If the cork is covered with a wax seal, just stick the corkscrew through the wax, pretending that it is not there, but brush away any stray pieces of wax before opening bottle.

❖ If your cork is fragile, use a two-pronged wine opener.

❖ If the cork breaks, reinsert the worm at a 45-degree angle into the remaining cork to work it out. Larger bottles have thicker corks, which can be more difficult to remove. These corks are also more likely to dry out, as these bottles may not have been stored on their sides.

How to Decant

❖ An important aspect of formal wine service, the decanting of wine serves two purposes. It allows the wine to breathe, or aerate, intensifying its flavors and aromas; and it also separates the bitter sediment in older wines.

❖ To decant, pour wine slowly into a clean glass or crystal decanter or pitcher and allow to rest about fifteen minutes before pouring.

❖ Many wine lovers advocate that careful decanting can improve almost any wine. And, of course, it looks more beautiful encased in crystal.

❖ Decanting older wines to separate the sediment is more complicated. To make sure that no sediment is poured, be sure that the bottle has been in an upright position for at least several hours before pouring very slowly into the decanter. Pouring against a good light helps to ensure that no sediment escapes. The wine remaining with the sediment can be strained with a coffee filter or discarded.

How to Taste

❖ If you order a bottle of wine, your sommelier or server will bring it to you for tasting.

❖ First, quickly read the label for varietal, vintage, and producer to be sure it is the wine you ordered. The labeling on the cork should match the label on the bottle.

❖ Once the bottle has been opened, inspect the cork to ascertain that it is intact and neither wet nor dry: There should be a trace of wine at the bottom of the cork. (Although movies often portray wine connoisseurs sniffing the cork, most would say that this behavior identifies a novice.)

❖ Indicate your approval to the server, who will then pour a small sample into your glass. Lift the glass to observe the wine's color and clarity and briefly sniff for vinegary or musty smells.

❖ Next, swirl the wine, keeping the bottom of the glass against the table, increasing and releasing the aroma. You can continue to swirl the wine while enjoying its aroma before sipping it. If the wine meets with your approval, you or the server will serve guests of honor, women, and older persons first, and you last.

How to Serve

❖ The best way to appreciate the color of wine is in a stemmed glass of plain, transparent crystal.

❖ The wine glasses at each place indicate the number of different wines to be served.

❖ Shapes of standard wine glasses have evolved to enhance the bouquet and maintain the correct temperature. Thus, traditionally, red wine glasses have the largest bowl and white wine glasses are smaller and tulip-shaped.

❖ Wine is served from the right before each course and replenished as needed.

❖ At a buffet, wine is usually offered when each guest is seated.

To Pour

❖ Pour slowly toward the center of the glass, filling it up to slightly below half way, leaving space for guest to swirl the wine.

- ❖ To prevent dripping, finish by tilting the lip of the bottle upward while slightly and quickly rotating your hand.

To Refuse

- ❖ Quietly say, "No, thank you" to the server or inconspicuously place your hand over the rim of the glass.

How to Drink

- ❖ Hold white wines by the stem to prevent the transfer of heat from your hand

- ❖ You may hold red wine by the bowl.

- ❖ Sip—don't gulp!

How to Store

- ❖ Unopened bottles are best kept in a cool place away from direct sunlight.

- ❖ They should be stored on their sides so that the wine keeps the cork bottom moist and the bottle airtight.

- ❖ Opened bottles can usually be stored in the refrigerator for up to four days without affecting the wine's taste.

- ❖ Remove the bottle from the refrigerator with enough time for it to warm up to its optimal temperature before serving.

WHAT NOT TO DO

- ❖ Serve white wines too cold or red wines too warm.

- ❖ Fill wine glasses to the rim.

❖ Turn your wine glass upside-down to indicate that you do not wish for any wine.

❖ Use the refrigerator to store wine, as potassium bitartrate crystals may develop, adversely affecting its taste.

CHAMPAGNE AND OTHER SPARKLING WINES

*W*ines *"sparkle" from natural fermentation or from injected carbon dioxide. The fizzy effervescence of sparkling wines appeals to many tastes, and wines can be white, rose, or red and range from very dry (brut) to very sweet (doux). They are produced in almost every country that makes wine. Some are named for the towns or regions in which they are produced (Asti, Champagne) and some for their grapes (prosecco). Much of the sparkling wine that is called champagne is not made with the same techniques as true champagne and takes only a few months rather than years to make.*

Although champagne as we know it was not produced until the 1800s, the process for creating sparkling wine has been evolving since the early 1500s. Today, there are several different methods of injecting carbon dioxide, all of which are quicker and less costly than the méthode champenoise ("Champagne method").

The quality of sparkling wine is judged by its mousse (bubbly foam), its perlage (size of bubbles streaming to the top, the smaller the better), the persistence of bubbles, and the mouth feel. Vintage blends use the yield of a single year's harvest. Cuvées de prestige, the finest champagnes, use only the best grapes from the best vineyards.

How to Chill

❖ Place wines in the refrigerator overnight or for at least three hours before opening. Remember that warm champagne is more dangerous to open than chilled.

❖ For last-minute chilling, put in a bucket with water, ice, and a little salt for about thirty minutes to chill to about 50 degrees. The salt helps to reduce the temperature.

How to Open

- ❖ Dry the bottle.

- ❖ Remove foil from the wire cage, keeping the cork pointed away from people.

- ❖ Undo the wire cage that encases the cork.

- ❖ Hold the cork (a towel can be used here) with one hand while slowly turning the bottle with the other until the cork begins to free up. The cork should not pop loudly, but sigh quietly.

How to Serve

- ❖ To reduce the exposed surface area, sparkling wines are usually served in glasses with a narrow opening, such as flutes or tulip glasses. This shape helps to conserve the bubbles.

- ❖ Although usually served alone, sparkling wines combine well with different juices and flavors and are used in many cocktails.

How to Pour

- ❖ Wrap the neck of the bottle with a clean towel or cloth.

- ❖ Hold the base in one hand, with your thumb in the punt (the concave bottom) and fingers spread out along the barrel of the bottle. Use your other hand to support the neck.

- ❖ Prime the glass by pouring a bit on the inside wall of the glass, wait for the mousse to temper and then pour more. Little bubbles should come to the surface. This indicates that there is nothing wrong with the wine and the glass has no contaminants on it. It also prevents frothing over. Pour to about two-thirds full. If pouring for several people, pour an inch or so into each glass, and then go around again.

How to Store

❖ Champagne must be kept under 60 degrees. The ideal temperature range is 53 to 59 degrees—the cooler the better.

❖ The place of storage should be dark, humid, and free of vibrations.

WHAT NOT TO DO

❖ Put sparkling wines in the freezer.

❖ Pop cork when removing.

❖ Store in the refrigerator for a long time.

❖ Turn the bottle when opening. Turn only the cork.

After-Dinner Coffees

*Only Irish coffee provides in a single glass all four
essential food groups: alcohol, caffeine, sugar, and fat.*

—Alex Levine

Coffee served at the conclusion of a multicourse dinner is intended to aid in digestion and to dispel the effects of alcohol from earlier cocktails and wines. After-dinner coffee service can be simple or elaborate, with or without alcohol, and poured into cups or glasses.

WHAT YOU NEED TO KNOW

❖ After-dinner coffees are traditionally served at the end of the meal—*after dessert.* In less formal settings, coffee is frequently served with the dessert course, as some believe it "cuts" the sweetness of the dessert. Some hosts offer it at both times.

❖ Coffee may be served at the dining table after the plates have been removed or in another room, such as a sitting room, library, living room, porch, or veranda.

❖ The size of the after-dinner coffee cup is determined by the strength of the brew. The stronger, richer and thicker the coffee, the smaller the cup. Thus, thick, heavy-bodied brews, such as espresso, are served in a smaller demitasse (half-cup) with correspondingly small saucer. At the table, the cup is placed to the right of the place setting.

❖ After-dinner coffees are often flavored with liqueurs, and some, such as Irish coffee, are poured into glasses and enhanced with sugar and whipped cream. Chocolate, peppermint, amaretto, and Irish cream are other popular flavors.

WHAT YOU MAY WANT TO KNOW

❖ Used mainly for informal dining, after-dinner coffee is served with an after-dinner coffee spoon. Following a more formal luncheon or dinner, the demitasse is served with a small demitasse spoon for stirring. Tongs may be used for serving cubed sugar. Small stirrers made of sugar or chocolate may also be provided.

❖ If there are no servers, the host usually pours at the table or from a tray.

❖ In certain business settings, such as in some Spanish-speaking countries, business is not discussed until coffee is served after the meal.

WHAT YOU MAY FIND HELPFUL TO KNOW

❖ It is usually preferable to complete the dessert course at the table before moving to another location for coffee, as it can be difficult (and potentially messy) for guests to balance both food and drink in their laps.

- ❖ The demitasse spoon is also known as a mocha spoon when it is used to stir a mixture of hot chocolate and coffee.

- ❖ When preparing Irish coffee, first temper the container. Heat the glass either by holding it over steam or by filling it with hot water before pouring in the hot coffee.

WHAT NOT TO DO

- ❖ Use a regular-size spoon in a demitasse cup.

- ❖ Request cappuccino as an after-dinner drink.

- ❖ In Italy or France, order any milky coffee after noon or with a meal. Milk beverages after a meal slow down the digestive process, whereas a water-based drink aids digestion.

CIGARS

A woman is only a woman, but a good cigar is a smoke.

–Rudyard Kipling

Cigar smoking is a culture in itself. The true cigar aficionado savors his unhurried indulgence for its complex aromas and subtle flavors. In order to appear cigar-worldly and experienced, you must learn how to choose, cut, light, smoke, extinguish, store, and truly enjoy the rituals and the smoke.

WHAT YOU NEED TO KNOW

Not all cigars are made the same. Look for handmade cigars, which are displayed and kept in a humidor.

How to Choose a Cigar

❖ The length and diameter are related to the intensity, thus a longer, thinner cigar results in a cooler smoke—one which would not cause the novice to cough.

❖ Darker wrappers indicate a full-bodied, stronger smoke with complex flavors, whereas lighter ones produce a milder smoke.

- ❖ To verify the quality, ask whether the cigar consists of 100 percent tobacco, squeeze slightly to ascertain that there are no lumps in it, check the end for discolored tobacco, and avoid cigars with stained wrappers.

- ❖ Select for taste, aroma, and visual aesthetics.

Parts of a Cigar

- ❖ Foot: The end meant to be lit.

- ❖ Head: The end closest to the cigar band that goes into the smoker's mouth.

- ❖ Tobacco: Dried and fermented leaves.

- ❖ Wrapper: Tobacco leaf spirally wrapped around the tobacco.

- ❖ Cigar band: The loop of paper or foil that identifies the brand and type of cigar.

- ❖ Tuck: The end of the wrapper that is folded in to keep it from undoing.

- ❖ Cap: A round of tobacco used to seal the head and keep it from drying out.

How to Cut

- ❖ There are three types of cuts: the straight cut (made with a single- or double-blade guillotine or with scissors) the punch cut (made with a bullet, Havana, or multi-punch device); and the V-cut (made with V-cutters, which cut a wedge into the cigar cap). There is also a cigar cutter and holder that takes off one end of the cigar and then acts as a holder for the fingers and thumb, securing the cigar.

❖ When cutting your cigar, use a very sharp blade—double guillotine is best—because jagged edges can result in uneven burning of the tobacco. Remove as little of the cap as possible and avoid cutting into the body of the cigar.

How to Light

❖ Hold the cigar between your index finger and thumb. If using a wooden match, wait for the sulfur to burn off. Taking your time, hold the cigar horizontally and then bring the flame to meet the end. When the flame is almost touching, draw slowly and lightly, rotating the cigar so that the end becomes uniformly charred. Blow gently on the end, if needed, for evenness. An even light is one of the most important aspects of smoking a cigar.

❖ Aficionados use many different techniques to light their cigars. Each method has its own devotees and experts. Popular nontraditional lightings include the Roll, Puff, and Blow; the Three Matches Method; the Flame Thrower; and the Torch/Match Switch-A-Roo.

How to Smoke

❖ Smoke slowly and do not draw frequently—about a puff a minute. If you draw too frequently, the heat will spoil the taste. Allow the flavorful smoke to drift around in your mouth for a few seconds—and enjoy.

❖ Large cigars can take hours to smoke. If your cigar stops burning before you have finished, make the ash fall and light the end of the wrapper. Next, exhale to push out the cold smoke and light up your cigar again. After two hours, most cigars acquire the unpleasant taste of cold smoke.

❖ Flick, but do not shake your cigar to make the ash fall prematurely. The better the cigar has been made, the longer the ash. However, if you let it become too long, it obstructs the airflow.

When and How to Extinguish

❖ You can smoke it far as you wish, depending on the taste. When the cigar begins to leave an aftertaste in your mouth, it is time to put it down. Gently blow through the cigar to expel any smoke and then simply set it aside in the cigar ashtray.

❖ After it extinguishes itself, dispose of the butt as soon as possible so that it doesn't give off the strong chemical odor of cold tobacco. Enjoy a libation that complements the flavors of your cigar.

How to Store

❖ Humidors, whether case, cabinet, or rooms, are usually made of cedar because it is most effective in controlling humidity. Keeping cigars at a constant humidity level helps them to retain moisture balance and to age well.

❖ The most popular choice, Spanish cedar, also has a strong smell, which drives away tobacco worms. American red cedar, a less expensive alternative, does not absorb moisture as well as Spanish cedar.

❖ Mahogany is also used for its humidity-fighting capability; however, it does not keep tobacco worms away.

❖ Do not store your cigars in the freezer or refrigerator, as the cold will retard the aging process and damage the tobacco.

WHAT YOU MAY WANT TO KNOW

❖ Cigars are classified based on where they are made and the tobacco leaves used. Major types include Churchill, Corona, Pyramid, Robusto, Torpedo, Panatelas, Celebras (three Panatelas braided together to form one cigar), Diademas, and the Perfecto.

❖ Carefully select the drink to accompany your cigar. The more full-flavored the cigar, the stronger the drink. Port, brandy, single-malt Scotch, rum, Kahlua, and coffee drinks can accompany most cigars.

❖ Cigars kept at high temperature and humidity levels can result in the hatching of tobacco beetles, which can then infest and eat through the cigars. (yuck)

❖ Cigars are hygroscopic in nature: they release and absorb moisture from the environment.

❖ The hobby of collecting vintage cigar bands is known as *vitolophily*.

❖ You can join the ranks of Cary Grant, Fred Astaire, Dean Martin, Frank Sinatra, and even Hugh Hefner! To absorb the smoke and protect your clothing from falling ash, invest in a smoking jacket. The epitome of elegant and comfortable at-home dressing, the traditional mid-thigh length smoking jacket is designed with loose cuffs, a shawl collar, a tie belt, and sometimes fasteners. It is usually made of silk and/or velvet; however, some more modern renditions are made of fabrics like corduroy and can be brightly patterned. In 1966 Yves St. Laurent created the famous Le Smoking look for women.

Machine-Made Cigars

❖ A cigarillo (sometimes called the seven-minute cigar) is a short, narrow cigar, which is usually machine-made and is smoked in quantities similar to cigarettes. They often come packed in ornately designed tins and need not be stored in humidors. As with cigars, breathe in to enjoy the taste, but do not inhale.

❖ A cheroot/stogie is clipped at both ends during manufacture (thus not tapered). It can be produced mechanically and purchased inexpensively. The word "stogie" is sometimes used colloquially to refer to a foul-smelling cigar.

WHAT YOU MAY FIND HELPFUL TO KNOW

❖ Because of the restrictive Cuban Trade Embargo, US citizens cannot legally acquire or consume Cuban cigars, even while traveling abroad. There are substantial fines and penalties for violators.

❖ Most tobaccos are blended to give the most enjoyment. Today almost the only unblended cigar is the Cuban.

❖ The wrapper, which is responsible for 60 percent or more of the cigar's flavor, consists of the outermost leaves of the tobacco plant. Wrapper leaves come in many species with variations in color and veins, and the novice is well advised to learn the terminology and to taste-test various wrappers as well as blends. A toothy wrapper is desirable because of the additional flavor that comes from pockets of oil that develop on the leaf, forming small bumps. To reduce the likelihood of the wrapper leaf's becoming damaged when removing a stuck band, some smokers leave the band on for a minute after lighting before removing it.

❖ For double enjoyment, pair music with your cigar. Often associated with smoky rooms, jazz is frequently the music of choice—and, naturally, almost all forms of Latin music are appropriate. Some albums are titled and marketed for the cigar smoker—and then there is Pink Floyd's classic, *Have a Cigar*.

❖ If you discover that you do not like your cigars, you can at least use the box to make your own cigar box guitar.

Cigar Bar/Lounge Etiquette

❖ Cigar smoking can be a solitary pursuit or a social event. Because many nonsmokers find cigar smoking to be obnoxious, smokers have difficulty finding places where they can enjoy the company of others. Most cigar lounges are in cigar stores, and some are in private clubs; however, all have unwritten rules. If in a store, make friends with the personnel (who are the most knowledgeable persons there), buy from the shop where you are smoking, and do not bring in cigars purchased from another purveyor. Do not talk on the phone or use the lounge as your office or living room. Respect others' cigar and drink choices, and don't offer "advice." Remember that Cuban cigars are banned by law.

Cigar Accoutrements for Aficionados

❖ Cigar Cutters (for handmade cigars): The most-used cutters are guillotines, a blade set into a frame with a hole that the cigar head fits into. The sharp blade cuts through the cigar head, leaving about an eighth of an inch of the cap remaining. To avoid tearing or pinching, proper technique calls for decisiveness and a firm grip close to the head of the cigar with a slight twist as the blade cuts through. To ensure a clean cut, use soap and water to clean your cutting blades.

Lighters and Matches

❖ Using spills (cedar strips/dividers found separating the layers of cigars in a box) for lighting adds both aroma and ritual to lighting the cigar.

❖ Special cigar matches light up more slowly.

❖ Use a butane lighter, not gas. For some smokers, even butane leaves a taste.

❖ Torch lighters are especially effective with certain lighting techniques.

Cigar Ashtrays

❖ Although they come in many shapes, colors, and designs, cigar ashtrays differ from conventional ashtrays in size and proportion. They must accommodate large amounts of ash as well as hold single or multiple cigars in place. Select for ease of cleaning and indoor or outdoor use.

Humidors

❖ Although cigars and personal preferences vary, the optimal environment for storing most cigars is 70 percent relative humidity and 70 degrees Fahrenheit. The humidor is designed to keep the humidity consistent and at the proper level. Available in all sizes and designs, humidors range from small leather travel cases to walk-in rooms and vaults. They can be designed within end tables, armoires, lockers, or display cabinets. The more elaborate walk-ins are lined with cedar and boast rolling ladders.

Humidifiers and Hydrometers

❖ Active humidifiers are common in large and walk-in humidors, whereas passive humidifiers are sufficient for smaller humidification needs. Always use distilled water in the humidifier that produces the humidity inside the humidor. You may wish to use an analog or digital hygrometer to measure your humidor's humidity level. Because the oils carry the flavors, the cigar's taste vanishes as the oils dry out. A dry cigar may be re-humidified, but the flavor itself cannot be replaced.

Water Pillow Cigar Humidor

❖ Inexpensive and useful if you are concerned that your cigar may dry out. A ziplock bag also works for a short time.

If you kiss a cigar, it will kiss you back. If you treat it like a dog, it will turn around and bite you.
                    –George Brighten, cigar guru

WHAT NOT TO DO

❖ Compromise the quality of a good cigar by lighting or smoking it incorrectly.

❖ Use scissors to cut off the end.

- ❖ ~~Use cheap matches to light it.~~

- ❖ Allow the flame to touch the tobacco.

- ❖ Inhale.

- ❖ Smoke the entire cigar at once.

- ❖ Show off the brand of your cigar by leaving the label on.

- ❖ Hold the cigar like a cigarette.

- ❖ Use a gas lighter, as it will affect the taste.

- ❖ Flick the cigar to make the ash fall prematurely.

- ❖ Crush the cigar (like a cigarette) on the ashtray. Let it go out on its own.

- ❖ Tell someone else how to smoke or insist that others will enjoy your choices more than their choices.

- ❖ Expose cigars to sun or heat.

- ❖ Try to bite the tip off unless you have practiced, as it works consistently only in old films.

I even smoke in bed. Imagine smoking a cigar in bed,
reading a book. Next to your bed, there's a cigar table with
a special cigar ashtray, and your wife is reading a book
on how to save the environment.

–Raul Julia

PART THREE
GAMES
PEOPLE PLAY

GOLF

Eighteen holes of match or medal play will teach you more
about your foe than will eighteen years of dealing with
him across a desk.

–Grantland Rice, sportswriter

Referred to as the *"gentlemen's game"* for centuries, golf is an outdoor game in which players use a club to hit a small hard ball, using as few strokes as possible to reach the green and get the ball into a cup hundreds of yards away. Obstacles, such as tall grass, water holes, and sand traps, may be found along the way. More complicated, confusing, and demanding than the novice player might assume, its rules—both written and unwritten—go beyond the usual practices of sportsmanship. Famous golfing professional Gardner Dickinson said, "They say golf is like life, but I don't believe them. Golf is more complicated than that." The game's etiquette, for both players and spectators, is about respect for others involved in the event as well as an appreciation for the quality of the course itself.

As A Spectator

❖ Wear sneakers or spikeless golf shoes to walk miles on grass and to help prevent course wear and tear.

❖ Always be quiet when play is going on.

❖ Keep movements to a minimum when players are about to swing.

❖ Wait for all players to putt out (finish putting) before leaving the green area for the next tee. Each golfer deserves your respect.

❖ Stay inside the ropes.

As A Player

❖ Clothing varies. Both women and men wear golf shoes with soft spikes, and women wear knee-length skirts or skorts, Bermuda shorts, or pants. Men wear slacks or long shorts and shirts with sleeves and collars.

❖ Respect the rules and regulations of the course where you are playing.

❖ Treat your caddy with respect and consideration.

❖ Always replace or repair divots and let faster groups through.

❖ Repair ball marks and rake footprints from bunkers (sand traps).

❖ Let the winner of the previous hole tee off first at the next tee.

❖ Allow the player farthest away from the pin to hit first on each shot.

❖ Drive the golf cart with care.

WHAT YOU MAY WANT TO KNOW

As A Spectator

❖ Learn and follow the spectator rules and guidelines set down by the club and the association hosting the event. You can always ask one of the volunteers if you have a question.

❖ Show respect for other spectators by kneeling down if you are in the front row and by not moving in front of others who were waiting there first.

❖ Cell phones are prohibited by most tournaments and some clubs.

❖ Although colors never found in nature or in the office are sometimes (unfortunately) acceptable on the golf course, some clubs do favor more muted attire.

As A Player

❖ Try to play at a considerate, reasonable pace. For the purposes of calculating handicaps, turn in every score.

❖ Avoid offering bets but accept them if offered by your client or boss. Win generously, and pay promptly if you lose.

WHAT YOU MAY FIND HELPFUL TO KNOW

As A Spectator

❖ Medal play (stroke play) is a scoring system that involves counting the total number of strokes taken on each hole during a given round or rounds.

❖ Dress for the weather. Bring a hat, sunglasses, sunscreen, or umbrella—and possibly something to sit on.

❖ Become familiar with the list of prohibited items, which may include food and drink, large bags or items, cameras, bicycles, radios, televisions, lawn chairs and folding arm-chairs, signs, banners, etc.

❖ As you could be using a portable toilet, you might bring some sanitizing wipes.

❖ You may cheer a good shot but only in moderate fashion.

❖ Take water and snacks for a long day, if allowed.

As A Player

❖ In general, the host tips the caddie, but if you have a per-sonal caddie, you may tip your caddie even though you are a guest.

❖ If you are serious about playing the game, learn the intrica-cies of golf etiquette, such as how many practice swings to take before a tee shot, who takes the pin, and rules for the tee box and the green.

WHAT NOT TO DO

As A Spectator

❖ Talk while someone is playing a stroke.

❖ Ask for autographs during a player's rounds. At some events autographs are permitted only at certain times and places.

❖ Boo or heckle.

❖ Applaud a player's mistake.

❖ Run around a golf course while a tournament is being played.

As A Player

❖ Wear jeans, cut-offs, short shorts, or tank tops

❖ Ask opponents what club they hit.

❖ Walk across or cast shadow on another player's putting line.

❖ Talk business until the group members are settled into the game and are comfortable with one another—and/or if someone is facing a difficult shot.

❖ Slow down other players.

❖ Continue play when lightning is in the area.

When I die, bury me on the golf course so my husband will visit.

–Anonymous

TENNIS (LAWN TENNIS)

A perfect combination of violent action taking place in an atmosphere of total tranquility.

–Billie Jean King, about tennis

A hugely popular spectator sport worldwide, tennis is an Olympic sport that can be played by people of all ages. Although now commonly called simply tennis, it was originally called lawn tennis because the game was played on grass courts when it began in Victorian England. Whether played by two players (singles) or between two teams of two players each (doubles), the object is to use a strung racket to hit a ball over a net in such a way that the opponent is not able to score a return.

Unlike many other sporting events, tennis has its own set of spectator rules. Because it is a respectful game and quieter than most sports, many of them are meant to prevent distractions that might affect a player's concentration.

WHAT YOU NEED TO KNOW

❖ The novice spectator would benefit greatly from learning the rules of the game and scoring system before attending a first match.

❖ Take your seat as soon as the game starts. If you have not yet located or reached your seat, take a seat where you are. Do not stand up and walk during the game.

❖ Cheering and applause are welcome after a well-played point, long rally, or a win.

❖ The raised chair on one side of the court is for the officiating umpire (head judge), who has the final authority to make determinations. The umpire may be assisted by line or net judges.

❖ When a match is delayed because of weather or other external conditions, the game is resumed with the same score and players in the same places as when play was halted.

WHAT YOU MAY WANT TO KNOW

❖ Tennis players use eight basic shots: the serve, forehand, backhand, lob, drop shot, volley, half volley, and overhead smash.

❖ Considered to be the most prestigious tennis tournaments in the world, each of the four Grand Slam tournaments— the Australian Open, the French Open, Wimbledon, and the US Open—lasts for two weeks and is held annually. The other major popular tournaments include the Davis Cup, Hopman Cup, Fed Cup, and the Olympic Games.

❖ In professional play, there are five types of court surfaces. Each plays differently with regard to ball speed and height of bounce. Clay courts, grass courts, hard courts (asphalt, concrete, acrylic), carpet (including artificial turf), and wood courts all play faster indoors than outdoors.

- ❖ As a match is a continuous game, player breaks are permitted only when beyond the player's control and absolutely necessary.

WHAT YOU MAY FIND HELPFUL TO KNOW

- ❖ The International Tennis Federation promulgates rules and regulations and provides information about teams, players, and competitions. In addition to the pro circuit, it oversees competitions for juniors (under eighteen), seniors, and wheelchair players.

- ❖ Most large tennis events have security checks. Some communication devices and beverages are not allowed into the site.

- ❖ Lawn tennis was first played in Birmingham, England in the mid-1800s.

WHAT NOT TO DO

- ❖ Chat, eat, or make any noise during the game.

- ❖ Stand in the aisle or sit on the handrail when a game is in session.

- ❖ Applaud, cheer, or shout during a point or serve.

- ❖ Talk directly to players or referees during the match.

- ❖ Make complaints about "bad" calls.

- ❖ Laugh, jeer, or applaud after an error, as this is most disrespectful.

- ❖ Leave cell phones on.

LEXICON

BACKHAND: Stroke made with the palm of hand facing player, moving from left to right for right-handed players.

DROP SHOT: Shot hit so that it drops quickly after crossing the net.

FOREHAND: Stroke made with the palm of the hand facing the direction of the stroke, moving from right to left for right-handed players.

GRIP: The way a player holds the racket when hitting shots, affecting the angle of the racket face.

HALF VOLLEY: Hitting the ball just as it touches the ground.

LOB: High shot that clears the opponent, landing at back of court.

OVERHEAD SMASH: A hard return; the player hits the ball above his or her head.

RETURN: Stroke that sends (returns) the ball back to the other player.

SERVE/SERVICE: Stroke to start a point (putting ball into play), made by tossing the ball into the air and hitting it into the diagonally opposite box (part) of the court without touching the net.

VOLLEY: Striking the ball before it touches the ground.

The depressing thing about tennis is that no matter how good I get, I'll never be as good as a wall.

–Mitch Hedberg

Court Tennis

The real "sport of kings." A game of moving chess that combines the exactitude of billiards, the hand-eye coordination of lawn tennis, and the generalship and quick judgment of polo.

–Unknown

WHAT YOU NEED TO KNOW

What It Is

❖ What the British call "real tennis," or "royal tennis" is labeled "court tennis" in the United States. It is the game from which lawn tennis (tennis played on lawns, clay, dirt, cement, asphalt, concrete, wood, or a composition surface) developed in the late nineteenth century.

❖ The game is played in a court that is similar in shape and size to medieval monastery cloisters and castle courtyards and reminiscent of church architecture.

❖ The game comes replete with social traditions, including the preservation of sportsmanship and honor.

Who Plays It

❖ The game is played primarily by amateurs; however, an elite group of pros—both touring and club—play in professional tournaments worldwide.

❖ The game is still generally played by men, although there are some women champions.

Part of the allure of court tennis is that nobody plays it.
Gabe Kinzler, court tennis and squash professional

How It Is Played

❖ With racquets and balls on a court divided by a sagging net on an indoor concrete court, measuring 110 feet by 38 feet, surrounded by 30-foot walls that contain openings.

❖ The wooden racket is spindly and somewhat bent.

❖ A player hits the handmade ball of tightly wound cloth over the center net and plays the surface of the floor, walls, and ceiling to keep the ball out his opponent's reach while also playing the ball off walls and roof or hitting the ball into wall openings.

❖ A handicap system is used, and the scoring system is complex.

There are similarities to tennis: the object of the game, as in tennis, is to win "sets" of six games; however, there are many differences. The novice spectator will have some difficulty recognizing these differences and may wish to study the complicated rules of the game. Terminology is also baffling. Terms such as penthouse, dedans, tambour, giraffe, railroad, and "chase the door" add to the mystery of the game. When listening to the announcer, remember that the score of the player who won the last point is always announced first. This differs from tennis, where the server's score is always announced first.

WHAT YOU MAY WANT TO KNOW

Where It Can Be Played and Viewed

❖ There are only approximately fifty courts throughout the world, and until very recently a mere one thousand Americans played on one of the ten courts in the United States. All are either private courts or part of exclusive clubs. In October 2012, however, another club returned: the Racquet Club of Chicago celebrated the restoration of the club's original court tennis court with three days of festivities. The original court had been converted to a tennis facility during the Great Depression.

❖ Some courts have a glass wall that enhances the viewing experience for spectators.

❖ Each court has unique markings and symbols.

About the Tennis Court Oath

❖ A pivotal event during the early days of the French Revolution, the Tennis Court Oath was a pledge signed on June 20, 1789, using a tennis court as a conference room by 576 members of 577 of France's Third Estate, comprised of commoners, and some members of the Second Estate, comprised of the nobility. The Oath was both a revolutionary act and an assertion that political authority derived from the people and their representatives rather than from the monarch himself. The Bastille was stormed a month later on July 14, 1789.

The History of the Game

❖ Although its beginnings have been traced back to the fertility rites of the Egyptians and Persians—in which the ball was the symbol of fertility—the game of today is believed to have originated in medieval France as a pastime of monks and other ecclesiasts.

❖ The game of many of Europe's leading monarchs, it was played in the Louvre and at Versailles and is mentioned in literature more often than any other sport.

❖ The French Revolution was the death knell of the game in France, but in both France and England, the game became popular again in the 1800s.

❖ Although a few people apparently played the game in colonial America, it wasn't until 1876 that a private court was built in the Back Bay area of Boston.

Famous Players

❖ Napoleon, King Henry VIII, King John of Sweden, Duke of Wellington, Prince Edward, the Earl of Essex, George Lambert, Jay Gould II, George Plimpton, and Jeremy Howard.

❖ Legend has it that Henry VIII was playing court tennis when Ann Boleyn went to the block in the Tower of London.

WHAT NOT TO DO

❖ Confuse court tennis with tennis.

❖ Ask questions about the game during the match.

❖ Use cell phones during a match, leave or return during live play, try to coach or talk to players during match, or complain or correct a score.

The only game that can rank in the list of arts and crafts.
–The French Royal Academy of Science, 1767

CROQUET

*Alice thought she knew how to play croquet on the lawn
of a manor house but suddenly found that playing the
game in a completely different and surrealistic culture was
very difficult. Wonderland's curious croquet ground was
all ridges and furrows; the mallets were live flamingoes;
the balls were active hedgehogs; and the soldiers (playing
cards) doubled themselves up, standing on both hands
and feet to form the arches. She had great difficulty
managing her mallets, tucking them under her arm as
they kept twisting around to look up in her face. The
hedgehogs kept unrolling themselves, then crawling away.
And the distorted soldiers got up to wander the grounds.
Even the rules were different: instead of taking turns,
everyone played at once!*

–Lewis Carroll, *Alice in Wonderland*

WHAT YOU NEED TO KNOW

❖ Croquet is an age and gender-neutral outdoor sport in which players use long-handled mallets to hit wooden or plastic balls through a series of hoops (wickets).

❖ The game is played on a rectangular lawn, or greensward, with precisely placed stakes and wickets.

❖ Although there are several variations of the game, the primary object is to be the first player to hit the ball through all of the wickets to reach a peg at the end.

❖ A social game that lends itself to casual and elegant entertaining, late nineteenth-century croquet was the raison d'etre for major parties, picnics, champagne suppers, and dancing.

❖ Today some major contests include nostalgic croquet balls (as in dances), dinners, picnics, and various charity events as part of the social scene. Tradition at certain formal croquet events dictates the pairing of tennis shoes with dinner jackets for the gentlemen.

❖ Traditional dress for players is all-white attire and flat-soled shoes. The United States Croquet Association rules still require all-white clothing in all USCA titled events. Some clubs are less strict, permitting the wearing of light beige shorts or pants, for example.

❖ For spectators, hats or sunshades as well as soft-soled shoes or sneakers are convenient, comfortable, and expected. Spectators should avoid distracting or conversing with board keepers or clock keepers, as their concentration is important to the game.

❖ The two most common forms of croquet are golf croquet and association croquet. Golf croquet is simpler, faster-paced (balls are more likely to go up off the ground), and has fewer rules. In golf croquet, each turn is a single shot.

Association croquet, played at an international level, is an advanced form of the game that is more complex, slower paced, and has additional rules. Extra turns are awarded for certain passes and hits. Its distinguishing feature is the "croquet shot," and its handicap system gives less experienced players a chance of winning against more accomplished opponents. A "bisque" is a handicap turn.

❖ Whether spectator or player, you should be familiar with certain conventions that apply in matches between clubs and at tournaments:

   o Players must stand off the court when an adversary is playing.

   o To play deliberately slowly in a timed game is considered cheating.

   o Holding a mallet, head up, above the head is a summons of a referee. Holding a mallet horizontally above the head is a summons of an umpire or assistant referee.

   o Traditionally, the lower handicap player tosses the coin at the start of each game.

   o A player cannot accept advice from anyone.

WHAT YOU MAY WANT TO KNOW

❖ The word "croquet" comes from the French word *crochet*, meaning "crooked stick."

❖ A full-length game of association croquet can take from one to three hours, depending on the skill of the players. A game of golf croquet takes less than an hour.

- Hitting another ball in association croquet is called a "roquet." A roquet sets up a "croquet" stroke.

- A deadness board displays the "dead" status of each player in respect to each other's player or color. Some boards are remotely controlled and operable by the players.

- The United States Croquet Association, located in Florida, has more than two hundred affiliated clubs in major cities, and many colleges have croquet clubs as well.

- Although the ideal backyard court is 50 feet wide by 100 feet long, these specifications can be scaled down; and whatever the size and placement of stakes and wickets, the grass should be cut as short as possible.

WHAT YOU MAY FIND HELPFUL OR INTERESTING TO KNOW

- The game was probably first played in Ireland and became very popular in Britain in the late nineteenth century.

- The croquet competition at the 1900 Olympic Games in Paris was not a spectator success, attracting only one fan. This Olympic event has not been repeated since.

- The major association croquet–playing countries are the United States, Canada, the United Kingdom, Ireland, Australia, and New Zealand.

- Traditional balls were made of wood, but most modern balls are made of heavy plastic.

- Ambassador Averell Harriman, so the story goes, refused to accept the post in the Soviet Union unless a croquet court was installed on the embassy lawn. Soviet scientists found that playing croquet had a calming, relaxing effect on their cosmonauts.

❖ Extreme croquet is played throughout the world in challenging locations that may include having to deal with mud, trees, roots, moving water, etc. The rigors of extreme croquet have resulted in the development of stronger mallets, balls, and wickets for this challenging game.

❖ Gateball, a croquet variant, originated in Japan and is popular in East and Southeast Asia.

❖ Norman Rockwell depicted the game in several of his paintings, including *Croquet.*

❖ H. G. Wells uses croquet as a metaphor for the way in which man encounters the problems of fear, distrust, and his own existence in *The Croquet Player.*

WHAT NOT TO DO

❖ Stand in a player's sight line.

❖ Take a long time to play your stoke.

❖ Tell opponents that they are about to hit the wrong ball or approach the wrong hoop.

❖ Wear clothing other than white to play in a tournament.

❖ Stroll about the croquet court using your long skirt to move the balls.

BACCARAT

My idea of gambling is to do it in a nice place with nice chandeliers, where people are elegantly dressed and there is champagne. If I am in love or doing a movie, I never think of the baccarat tables. When I am bored though, it's often all I can think about.

–Omar Sharif

A favorite of French and Italian nobles from as early as the fifteenth century, the game of baccarat still epitomizes sophistication, high stakes, and elegance. Its gamblers follow a code of behavior as well as rules of play. Highly visible players, including James Bond in Casino Royale, Sean Connery, Michael Jordan, and Akio Kashiwagi, contribute to its mystique. Baccarat players and observers are expected to be knowledgeable and courteous at all times, contributing to the game's image.*

WHAT YOU NEED TO KNOW

❖ Baccarat is not a game of skill. It has a low house edge, and the rules are simple. It is usually played in a separate room or cordoned-off area. It is a casino card game dealt from a shoe.

❖ The object of the banking game is to form a hand whose point value is closer to nine than the hand of the banker.

❖ You should dress for the game, checking to see what players are wearing. You will probably not be allowed to enter the game area if you are wearing casual clothing.

❖ In American play, there are two kinds of tables: the long traditional tables, seating up to fifteen players and three dealers and the blackjack-style mini tables with seven players and one dealer.

❖ After entering the room, walk around observing the game and its flow for a few minutes before sitting. Some casinos may have only a few active tables. Table minimums are usually posted at each table. Sit at a table where the game is almost finished or is just beginning. Smile at other players—light banter is common.

❖ Once the bet is made, do not touch or adjust it in any way.

WHAT YOU MAY WANT TO KNOW

❖ Baccarat is an unhurried game, and players act slowly and deliberately—not quickly or impulsively.

❖ If you wish to take a break, simply indicate this. The dealer will take care of your chips.

❖ Do not be in a hurry to collect your earnings. Wait until others have received theirs.

❖ When cashing out, trade in a large number of smaller chips for large ones.

- ❖ Baccarat was derived from the French game *chemin de fer* and the Italian game *punto banco*. Baccara means "zero" in both languages.

- ❖ Baccarat came to Las Vegas in 1959.

WHAT YOU MAY FIND HELPFUL TO KNOW

- ❖ If you are asked to handle the shoe (dealing box) and do not feel comfortable doing so, it is appropriate etiquette to politely decline. Other players or the dealer will do it instead.

- ❖ Dealers often pay winners with the highest denomination possible.

- ❖ Do not waste playing time by asking the dealer for lots of lower denomination chips.

- ❖ Making a side bet for the dealer is a nice gesture.

WHAT NOT TO DO

- ❖ Crash a baccarat table.

- ❖ Immediately ask what the table minimum is.

- ❖ Formally introduce or announce yourself.

- ❖ Interrupt a hand during play.

- ❖ Forget to tip the dealer.

- ❖ Complain when you lose. If you can't afford to lose, don't bet.

PART FOUR

HORSE COUNTRY

POLO

Playing polo is like trying to play golf during an

earthquake.

–Sylvester Stallone

O ne of the roughest, fastest, and most dangerous sports played today, the equestrian "game of kings." is an easy and exciting game and event for a first-time spectator to enjoy.

WHAT YOU NEED TO KNOW

About the Game

- ❖ Field polo is played on horseback between two teams of four players each.

- ❖ Players use long-handled mallets (measuring fifty-one inches) to score points by driving wooden or solid plastic ten-inch balls between the opponent's goal posts.

- ❖ Teams switch ends after each goal.

- ❖ It is played on a ten-acre grass field with goal posts at each end. The playing field is called the pitch.

❖ Each rider requires several ponies (horses) throughout the game. These are called the polo string.

❖ A polo match lasts about two hours and is divided into six seven-minute periods called chukkers with four minutes between each. There is a ten-minute halftime. The polo season runs from April through September.

❖ Most seating is in grandstand or bleacher-type seating. Some have exclusive members' areas or enclosures or VIP tents. Grandstand viewers frequently tailgate or eat a picnic on the surrounding lawn, while members and VIPs may be served a lavish luncheon.

❖ Arena polo, or indoor polo, is obviously more restricted in space and thus has shorter plays and lower speeds than field polo. Arena polo has three players per team and players frequently play the game with only one pony, making it a much less expensive sport. In the United States and Canada, collegiate polo is arena polo.

Stomping the Divots

❖ Polo spectators have the unique opportunity to become an interactive part of the game when they "stomp the divots," or are "treading in." During halftime and sometimes at other breaks, onlookers are invited to wander the field and stomp down the torn up turf. A very social part of the event, sometimes even the players join in stomping to keep themselves limber.

Attire

❖ Although a wide range of dress is acceptable, there is an etiquette surrounding appropriate attire. The type of match you are attending will determine your dress. Informal games and preliminary matches are smart casual.

❖ For finals or championship games men usually wear jackets and women wear dresses.

❖ Spectators at national-level games and classic major tournaments follow a more formal dress code, with men in suits and women in elegant dresses and fanciful hats.

❖ Major tournaments and special charity events each have their own pageantry and social conventions and may come replete with time-honored traditions such as elaborate brunches, afternoon tea, or art auctions. Some are by invitation only.

WHAT YOU MAY WANT TO KNOW

❖ Players always wear white riding pants and a polo shirt (of course), helmets, high boots, knee guards, and gloves.

❖ The horses, called polo ponies, are actually thoroughbred or mixed-breed horses. They reach their peak around nine or ten years of age.

❖ Polo ponies require lots of training, conditioning, and exercising.

❖ Because the field is large, it is wise to bring your binoculars.

❖ A trumpet is part of the tradition; however, the horses are accustomed to the blasts that signal goals and thus do not react. You should not react either.

❖ Polo matches are regulated by one or two umpires.

❖ Although still very male-dominated, more and more women are playing the sport and becoming recognized professionals and stars.

WHAT YOU MIGHT FIND HELPFUL TO KNOW

❖ Polo is unique among team sports in that amateur players hire and play with top professionals.

❖ Most polo clubs are open for public viewing on weekends, but you might wish to bring a blanket or folding chair.

❖ All polo players are assigned handicaps (ranking) according to ability.

❖ The tails of polo ponies are braided to prevent tangling with the mallets, and the mane is shaved ("roached" in the United States; "hogged" in the United Kingdom). Six different types of braids are used.

❖ Polo is played in more than sixty countries and enjoyed by more than 50 million people each year.

❖ Ancient Mongol warriors created polo to hone their battle skills.

WHAT NOT TO DO

❖ Plan to go divot stomping in high heels.

❖ Sit on the fences surrounding the polo pitch.

❖ Make sudden sounds that could frighten the horses.

❖ Shout for favorite players or when goals are made.

❖ Take photos during a match.

❖ Refer to the ponies as" horses."

❖ Park too close to the playing field.

Fox Hunting

*About fox hunting: the unspeakable chasing the
uneatable.*

– Oscar Wilde

Practiced all over the world and especially controversial in the
United Kingdom and the United States, fox hunting involves the
tracking, chasing—and sometimes killing—of a (traditionally
red) fox by trained scent hounds and a group of unarmed followers who
pursue on horseback or foot.

Fox hunting conventions and etiquette are based on traditions that go
back hundreds of years; though some of these rules have evolved to accommodate certain situations and fit the times, others remain rigidly conventional. Most of them address issues of safety, order, readiness, and sports-
manlike conduct and vary little from club to club.

WHAT YOU NEED TO KNOW

❖ Most importantly, know the rules of the hunt. First-time
riders should discuss them with an experienced member
of the field before hunting. If you invite guests, you are
responsible for their understanding and following of the
rules.

❖ The sport relies on a standard set of verbal and visual commands for reacting to various situations. Knowledge of these commands is essential.

❖ Be prepared—well trained, well mounted, and properly attired.

❖ Your horse and tack must be neat and clean. Your horse's mane must be plaited.

❖ Each hunt prescribes its own hunting attire. Follow instructions carefully. Novices will not be invited to wear the hunt club's colors. Even informal hunt attire is specific as to acceptable boots, jacket, and colors.

❖ Be prompt.

❖ The master is the final authority in the field and will address any behavior that is rude, unsafe, or unsportsmanlike.

❖ Remain silent during the presentation of the pack at which time the master or field masters may greet riders and make announcements.

❖ There is a traditional hunt field order, which most clubs follow. Take your proper position. You will be sharing your position in the field with others of the same rank and yielding to riders of greater seniority.

❖ Always give right-of-way to the master, hunt staff, and hounds.

❖ At the conclusion of the hunt, thank the master and his staff.

WHAT YOU MAY WANT TO KNOW

❖ Usually non-riding members and their guests, with proper instruction and supervision, may follow the hunt by car or on foot.

❖ Leave everything as you find it. If a gate is left open, do not shut it; if you take a rail down, put it back.

❖ A red ribbon on a horse's tail means that it has a tendency to kick.

WHAT YOU MAY FIND HELPFUL TO KNOW

❖ To insure that no one falls behind, is injured, or falls off his horse, newcomers and guests should use the "buddy system" when riding at the rear of the field.

❖ When hunting is over, the meal served is breakfast—no matter what time of day.

❖ The masters award "colors" to hunting members who have made ongoing significant contributions to the traditions of the hunt and sportsmanship.

WHAT NOT TO DO

❖ Refer to hunting hounds as dogs.

❖ Wear anything that could be caught on branches or other obstacles possibly causing injury to you, your horse, or others.

❖ Ride over crops, seeded fields, lawns, or flower beds. Stay to edges of fields or in the field rows.

- Pass the field masters.

- Jump a fence until all hounds are clear.

- Smoke.

- Lag behind.

- Make or receive calls except in an emergency situation.

LEXICON

COLORS: The colored collar and, usually, buttons that distinguish the uniform of a particular hunt.

COUPLE: Hounds are always counted in couples (i.e., five hounds equals two-and-a-half couples).

FIELD: Group of members and guests gathered to follow the hounds.

FIELD MASTERS: Person/s who lead the field during the hunt and are responsible for field while out hunting.

HUNTSMAN: Person who hunts hounds, using voice and horn, and who is responsible for their care, training, and breeding.

LINE: The trail of the fox.

MASTER OF FOXHOUNDS (MFH): Person responsible for the hunting, all decision-making, and of every facet of the hunt.

MEET: The actual place of the hunt.

NOSE: The hound's ability to detect and interpret a scent.

PACK: Hounds whose bloodlines have been selected to produce particular attributes (i.e., scenting ability, obedience, stamina, drive, voice, and desire).

TURNOUT: Foxhunting attire.

WHIPPERS-IN (WHIPS): Persons responsible for controlling the hounds and riding with the pack during a chase.

Horse Races and Race Meetings

Money, horse racing, and women: three things the boys just can't figure out.

–Will Rogers

An equestrian sport with a long history, horse racing, including char-iot racing, dates back to ancient Egypt and Syria as well as the first Pan-Hellenic games and the early Roman Empire. Thoroughbred racing became particularly popular with British royalty and aristocrats warranting it the title "king of sports."

Important races are premier social and sporting events at tracks through-out the world. The weekend's social calendar may include elegant black-tie balls, elaborate picnics, special functions, and charity events.

What You Need to Know

❖ Internationally, wherever thoroughbred racing is popu-lar, the Triple Crown of thoroughbred racing consists of three races for three-year-old thoroughbred horses. In the United States, the three races that comprise the Crown are the Kentucky Derby at Churchill Downs in Louisville, Kentucky; Preakness Stakes at Pimlico Race Course in Bal-timore, Maryland; and Belmont Stakes at Belmont Park in

Elmont, New York. All three are dirt tracks, with Belmont Stakes being the longest in thoroughbred racing.

❖ The foremost thoroughbred races in North America and the United Kingdom are notable occasions. Tradition, pageantry, and fashion all combine for an exhilarating atmosphere. In addition to the Triple Crown events, major US races, tracks, and events include the Breeders Cup World Championship, which changes venue each year; the Jockey Club Gold Cup, Belmont Park, Elmont, New York; the Charleston Cup (steeplechase), Charleston, South Carolina; Opening Day, Saratoga Race Course, Saratoga Springs, New York; Del Mar Thoroughbred Club, Del Mar, California; and Santa Anita Park, Arcadia, California.

❖ There are three major types of horse racing: steeple chasing—racing over hurdles/fences; harness racing—trotting horses pulling drivers in sulkies; and flat racing—running a predetermined distance on a level track. The flat race is the most common in North America.

❖ Fashion decorum is taken seriously. Spectators are expected to adhere to the conservative dress code in the area of the racecourse for which they are invited or have a ticket. More casual dress is acceptable and dress codes are seldom enforced in grandstand areas.

❖ Become conversant about horse racing and the betting procedures before attending your first race meeting. Unlike most other spectator sports, all racetrack activity takes place in just a few minutes, leaving long intervals with no sports action and many opportunities for social conversation and interaction.

WHAT YOU MAY WANT TO KNOW

❖ Between races, it is customary to people to get up and move around, parading from betting areas to parade ring to bars, etc. For some, this is an opportunity to display fashionable attire.

❖ American betting on horseracing is regulated by the state the racetrack is located in.

❖ Different areas and countries offer other types of horse racing, such as endurance racing and quarter horse racing.

❖ The first US endurance race began in California around 1955 and marked the beginning of the Tevis Cup. Most long-distance endurance races are fifty or one hundred miles in length. Competitive trail riding races are shorter, covering difficult terrains.

❖ Founded in 1711 by Queen Anne, the Royal Ascot in Berkshire, England, is a glamorous five-day event that is always attended by the Queen and other royals and notables who are seated in the exclusive Royal Enclosure. All attendees must adhere to strict dress codes that are published (and videotaped!) as well as enforced by dress code administrators. The code goes back to racing as a pleasure pastime for the elite and denotes respect for the monarchy. Women who arrive in sleeveless dresses may obtain a shawl at the door, and men who forget a tie may obtain one at the entrance.

❖ In terms of style, these prestigious race meetings are renowned for the women's display of flamboyant, beautiful, exotic—even outrageous—hats, and for star-studded events, black tie galas, and lavish picnics complete with silver service, candelabra, and butlers.

❖ Horses run in their owners' unique colors, which must be registered.

❖ The Golden Slipper, the richest race for two-year-old thoroughbreds, is Australia's premier race. It is held at the Rosehill Gardens Racecourse in Sydney.

WHAT YOU MAY FIND HELPFUL TO KNOW

❖ All North American thoroughbreds have birthdays set on January 1, regardless of their actual birthdays. They become yearlings when they reach their first August 1—even if they were born that July.

❖ There is a class system for North American racing horses: maiden races are for top quality horses who have not yet won a race; claiming races are for purchasing or claiming horses out of a race; allowance races are for non-winners who are allowed certain conditions that help to place them at a level where they have a chance to win; and stakes races (with three different grades) are for only the cream of the crop who bring the highest purses.

❖ Any horse that has not yet won a race is known as a maiden. To "break a maiden" means to win a first race.

❖ Getting admitted into the Royal Enclosure at Ascot (a quite large area) requires an application to the Royal Enclosure Office as well as the recommendation of a member who has attended the Royal Enclosure for at least four years.

- ❖ Male guests of the Royal Enclosure are required to wear black or grey morning wear, including waistcoat, tie, correct black shoes, and top hat, which must be worn at all times unless one is in a restaurant or private area. The top hat may not be customized with additions or colors.

- ❖ The fascinator, a (sort of) perennially popular head covering, is banned from the Royal Enclosure.

WHAT NOT TO DO

- ❖ Fail to comply with the dress code for your seating area.

- ❖ Bet if you cannot afford to lose the money.

- ❖ Gloat if you are a winner—just sit back and enjoy a quiet sense of satisfaction.

- ❖ Attempt to kiss while wearing a wide-brimmed hat.

<Begin formatting – text box>

LEXICON

BLINKERS/BLINDS: Headgear that prevents a horse from looking to the right or left.

COLT: Ungelded male horses of up to four years of age.

COURSE SPECIALIST: A horse that has either won or made good time on previous races.

DAM: A horse's mother.

DARK HORSE: Promising horse with unknown potential.

FURLONG: An eighth of a mile (220 yards).

JOCKEYS: Person (usually light in weight) who professionally races horses.

NURSERY: A handicap race for two-year-olds.

RACE CARD: Program listing races and names of horses running.

STALLION: Male ungelded horse that has never bred.

STUD: Male ungelded horse that has bred.

TACK: Equipment used in horseback riding, including bridle and saddle.

THOROUGHBRED: A breed originally developed in England from crosses between Turkish, Arabian, and existing English lines. They are used and bred mainly for racing and can be crossbred to create or improve existing breeds.

PART FIVE

TRAVELING IN STYLE

Yachting: Sail or Motor

Land was created to provide a place for boats to visit.

—Brooks Atkinson

W hether you are casual or formal, guest or crew, sailing or motoring, cruising or racing, in yacht club or fishing boat, safety and respect are the basis of most boating etiquette and protocol.

WHAT YOU NEED TO KNOW

❖ What to wear on board: Appropriate shoes, such as deck or boat shoes with non-marking, nonskid white soles, and comfortable, layered clothing.

❖ What to wear at yacht club: Respectful, appropriate attire in keeping with the formality of the specific club and/or occasion.

❖ What to bring: Soft, stowable luggage; windbreaker and/or sweater for chilly evenings.

❖ What to remember: Be on time, respect the sea, always obey the captain/skipper and follow boat rules, and learn the head (marine toilet) instructions and general nautical know-how.

WHAT YOU MAY WANT TO KNOW

❖ General nautical terms (see Lexicon).

❖ Basic sailing terms and maneuvers.

❖ Etiquette and rules for a specific yacht club, including saluting, uniforms, commodore, and vice commodore and nameplate etiquette.

❖ How much gratuity to tip the crew of your charter: ten to fifteen percent of charter fee is usually given to the captain to distribute.

WHAT YOU MAY FIND HELPFUL TO KNOW

❖ Whistle and horn signals.

❖ Right-of-way rules.

❖ Burgee and flag etiquette.

❖ The America's Cup: Founded in 1851, this sailing competition is the oldest active trophy in international sport.

❖ Rafting guidelines.

❖ Royal yacht clubs: In countries formerly part of the British Empire, many clubs boast the honorific "royal" in their titles. Their flag and yacht etiquettes are derived from the customs and usage of the Royal Navy.

WHAT NOT TO DO

❖ Climb aboard a boat before bring granted permission by the captain or crew.

- ❖ Enter the galley unless specifically invited.

- ❖ Waste fresh water.

- ❖ Invite someone on board without first asking the captain's permission.

- ❖ Board without appropriate medication (patch or Dramamine) if you tend to get seasick.

- ❖ Throw any garbage overboard.

- ❖ Put your electric appliance or magnetic potholder next to the boat's compass.

- ❖ Wear loose or dangling jewelry or scarves that could catch on something.

- ❖ Drink too much alcohol.

- ❖ Bring illegal drugs or firearms.

LEXICON

ABOARD: On or within a boat.

ABOVE DECK: On the deck, not over it.

AFT: Toward the stern or back of the boat.

AWEIGH: Raising the anchor clear of the bottom, as in "anchors aweigh!"

BELOW: Beneath the deck.

BOW: The forward part (front) of the boat.

BULKHEAD: Vertical partition separating compartments.

BUOY: Anchored float used to mark a location on the water; it can indicate a shallow or hazard or be used for mooring.

BURGEE: The distinguishing flag of a boating organization, usually a yacht club.

CABIN: Compartment used for passengers or crew.

CATAMARAN: A twin-hulled boat.

COCKPIT: An opening in the deck from which the boat is piloted.

COURSE: Direction in which a boat is steered.

DINGHY: Small open boat.

DOCK: Area in which vessels are moored, includes wharfs and piers.

DRAFT: The depth of water a boat draws.

FATHOM: Unit of measurement of water depth equal to six feet.

GALLEY: Kitchen area of a boat.

GUNWALE: Top edge of the side of a boat.

HATCH: Opening in a boat's deck fitted with a watertight cover.

HEAD: A boat/ship's toilet.

HELM: Wheel or tiller that controls the rudder.

HULL: Main body of a vessel.

JETTY: Structure, usually masonry, which projects out from the shore.

KNOT: Nautical measure of speed equal to one nautical mile (6,076 feet) per hour— equivalent to approximately 1.5 miles per hour.

LAUNCH: Skiff/boat run by marina or club to take you out to a moored boat.

LEE: Side of something sheltered from the wind.

LINES: Just means rope!

MOORING: Device, such as cables or lines, used to secure a boat to a buoy or pier; sometimes refers to the buoys themselves.

NAUTICAL MILE: Approximately 6,076 feet (about an eighth longer than the standard mile of 5,280 feet).

OUTBOARD: Detachable engine mounted on a boat's stern.

PILING: Support for wharves, piers, etc. constructed of poles (piles) driven into the bottom.

PORT: The left side of a boat when looking forward, toward the bow.

RUNNING LIGHTS: Lights are required to be shown on boats between sundown and sunup.

SLIP: Where boat ties up beside the dock, a club, marina, or private residence.

STARBOARD: The right side of a boat when looking forward, toward the bow.

STEM: The forwardmost part of the bow.

STOW: To put an object in its proper place on board.

TILLER: Bar or handle for turning a boat's rudder or an outboard motor.

UNDERWAY: Vessel in motion—traveling, not moored, anchored or aground.

WAKE: Waves or path that a moving boat leaves behind when crossing waters.

AIR ETIQUETTE: PRIVATE AIRCRAFT, HELICOPTERS, AND DIRIGIBLES/BALLOONS

The air up there in the clouds is very pure and fine, bracing, and delicious. And why shouldn't it be?—it is the same the angels breathe.

—Mark Twain, *Roughing It*

Whether for business or pleasure, in a rush or sightseeing, passengers on any charter, private craft, or special aircraft, are expected to understand the rules of polite and safe behavior. As the guest of an individual or corporation, your thoughtfulness, good manners and "jet-iquette" will contribute to a more comfortable flight in close quarters.

WHAT YOU NEED TO KNOW

❖ Inquire ahead of time about luggage restrictions—number, size, and weight.

❖ Dress comfortably. Avoid wearing very high heels and flip-flops. (Some helicopters and dirigibles/blimps prohibit them.)

❖ You are expected to arrive on time (usually no security lines or crowds). Private aircraft have scheduled departure times and being late could result in unnecessary fines for your host.

❖ Ask whether seats are assigned before selecting one: "Where would you like me to sit?" Follow ALL instructions from the pilot and crew.

Helicopters

❖ Do not approach or leave a helicopter until the pilot has signaled that it is okay for you to do so.

❖ While in flight, secure seatbelts and use helmet or headset if provided.

❖ Remain in your seat unless given permission to move.

❖ Read and follow all instructions.

❖ Wait for blades to come to a complete stop before exiting.

WHAT YOU MAY WANT TO KNOW

❖ The pilot is called pilot, not captain.

❖ The owner or person paying for the flight usually gets the best seat, so it is best to not take your seat until after the hosts have found theirs.

❖ The kitchen is called the "galley", and the bathroom is called the" lavatory."

❖ If you have the opportunity to sit in the front seat next to the pilot, lean away from the pilot, keeping your limbs away from the controls.

Helicopters

❖ There are usually no airsickness bags in helicopters.

❖ Secure your clothing, hats, and scarves, and carry gear firmly at your side, not over your shoulder or above your head.

WHAT YOU MAY FIND HELPFUL TO KNOW

❖ Bring reading material that can be shared.

❖ If you are the guest of a private host, show your thanks by bringing a gift—perhaps one that could be shared by all members of the group—or give a "good-for" card.

❖ Do not bring food or beverages aboard unless you are certain that meals will not be provided and that you are expected to bring your own, and then ascertain that there will be plates, cutlery, microwave, etc. available. Certain foods and drinks are sometimes prohibited in flight.

Hot-Air Balloons

❖ When landing a hot-air balloon, proper etiquette calls for offering the landowner a glass (or bottle) of champagne!

Helicopters

❖ You might want to bring an alcohol swab or use your hand cleanser to wipe off your headset's microphone.

WHAT NOT TO DO

❖ Be late for departure.

- Bring a small (or large) pet without an invitation; if invited, do not let the animal loose in the cabin.

- Use tobacco products, unless you are certain it is acceptable and that you won't offend other passengers.

- Tip the staff—that's up to the owner/host.

- Expect your host to entertain you during the flight.

- Wear heavy perfumes, fragrant lotions, or jangling jewelry.

- Bring heavy, bulky carry-on items.

- Use cell phones where prohibited—on or around aircraft.

- Go near the tail rotor of a helicopter.

- When taking photos, remember there will be little space in which to maneuver your equipment. Do not request the pilot to fly at unsafe altitudes or airspeeds.

- Express your anxiety, fears, or concerns about the trip to the crew, host, or fellow passengers.

PART SIX

RELIGIOUS SERVICES AND CEREMONIES

INTRODUCTION

We all meet, make friends, and work with people of many different religious backgrounds. However, our cultural competence is called into question when we attend an unfamiliar religious ceremony or enter an unfamiliar church or temple. North American communities of faith are many and varied, and each community has different sects and/or denominations. Our religious pluralism offers many different ways to pray, praise, rejoice, celebrate, marry, and mourn. The occasions for which you are most likely to receive an invitation—basic services, marriages, and funerals—are addressed here.

BUDDHIST

The greatest achievement is selflessness.

–Anonymous

B uddhist traditions vary widely depending on the teachings of different schools of thought and the country of origin. The essence of Buddhist practice is based in the Four Noble Truths: life is suffering, the origin of suffering is attachment, the cessation of suffering is attainable, and the true path to the cessation of suffering is the Eightfold Path.

Buddhists celebrate many festivals and holy days based on the lunar calendar and thus they vary not only by local tradition but also by date and time of year. However, the only festival that is celebrated by Buddhists worldwide is Wesak, or Buddha Day. In many traditions it is celebrated in May or June; in Zen Buddhism, Buddha Day is December 8. Wesak cards are exchanged and celebratory meals and services are enjoyed.

SERVICES AND CEREMONIES

For any event, guests will find it helpful to call the temple or to speak with the host prior to the visit to ask whether attendees will be seated in chairs or pews or on meditation floor cushions because this may determine dress. As many Buddhists are vegetarian or vegan, meals served to you may not *include animal products. Before hosting Buddhists, inquire about their food preferences.*

❖ **Basic Service**: In a Buddhist temple, a priest, monk, or temple president leads the service. A bell is used to indicate the beginning and end of meditation. An incense burner, placed in front of the altar, is offered to the Buddha.

❖ **Marriage Ceremonies:** As marriage is not a sacred Buddhist ceremony, and the purpose of the wedding is to remind those present to respect each other and live harmoniously with all sentient beings, it is a short civil ceremony usually followed by a blessing or celebration at a temple, outdoor setting, or other venue. If the blessing takes place in a shrine room, take off your shoes before entering. A bell or gong signals the start and end of the blessing.

❖ **Mourning and Funerals**: Because Buddhists believe that one enters one's next incarnation immediately after death, their mourning combines grief and bereavement with joy for the deceased. They often continue to be of service to others by donating their organs for medical or research use.

❖ Traditions vary. While most Japanese Buddhist funerals are held within one week, in other countries, such as Sri Lanka and Thailand, three different ceremonies are held for the deceased. Two days after death, monks hold a home service; a few days later, they hold a service at a funeral home. Seven days after the cremation or burial, a "merit transference" is held at home or temple. Condolence cards and flowers are appreciated, and donations are usually made to a charity or cause of the family's choice.

❖ At the ceremony, everyone stands as the coffin enters the room. The service may include meditation, chanting, prayers, music, and/or readings and includes the use of incense, candles, and bells. Temple services may last up to an hour; crematorium services are shorter. If there is a post-funeral gathering, you will be notified in advance.

❖ There are also rituals for observing anniversaries. Most take place ninety days or a year after the death.

DRESS

Although standards have become more casual, some temples still expect women to wear a dress or skirt and men to wear a jacket and tie. If you will be seated on floor pillows, wear suitable and comfortable clothing. No head coverings are required in a Buddhist temple. Clothing may be of any color for most occasions; however, most people wear dark clothing when attending a funeral.

PARTICIPATION

As a gesture of respect, practicing Buddhists bow slightly to monks and nuns, cupping their hands together into the shape of a lotus bud. They may also kneel, prostrating themselves in front of the Buddha's statue. Visitors are not expected to do either of these or to participate in any of the other rituals. If you wish to contribute to the temple, you will probably find an offertory box near the entrance.

WHAT NOT TO DO

❖ Point your feet toward the Buddha.

❖ Communicate with the bereaved or send food before a funeral.

❖ Enter or leave any service or ceremony during meditation.

❖ Talk or whisper during any service or ceremony.

LEXICON

DHARMA: Refers to Buddhist teachings.

KARMA: Cause and effect; what you do in this life affects your subsequent lives.

MALA: String of prayer beads used by priests, monks, and congregants.

MANTRA: Repetitive prayers.

NIRVANA: Peace of mind, a state free from all suffering and confusion.

SANGHA: Spiritual community.

ROMAN CATHOLIC

We are the Easter people, and hallelujah is our song.
— Pope John Paul II

The largest denomination of Christianity, the Roman Catholic Church is characterized by an Episcopal hierarchy with the pope as its head. Its basis for worship is the mass. Roman Catholic services are held on Sunday mornings as well as at other times throughout the week. Major holy days are Christmas, December 25; Ash Wednesday, forty days before Easter; Maundy/ Holy Thursday, four days before Easter; Good Friday, three days before Easter; Easter, the Sunday after the first full moon after the spring equinox; and Pentecost, fifty days after Easter. Catholics also celebrate life cycle events with baptisms for babies, confirmations, weddings, funerals, and interments.

When entering a Roman Catholic Church, the visitor will notice an area with candles on circular stands. Catholics light these votive offerings to give thanks or to ask that a prayer be answered. When entering and leaving the sanctuary, members will cross themselves with holy water and will then again make the sign of the cross while genuflecting before entering the pew. There will be both pews and chairs for seating as well as kneeling benches. Catholics may kneel for a short prayer before the Mass begins. Although the language of the Catholic Church in America is English, some Masses and weddings are performed in the dominant language of the neighborhood.

Traditional forms of address for clergy are "Father" for priests, "Your Excellency" for bishops, "Your Eminence" for cardinals, and "Your Holiness" or "Most Holy Father" for the Pope.

SERVICES AND CEREMONIES

❖ **Basic Service:** The Roman Catholic Mass begins and concludes with a procession led by a church member carrying a cross, followed by the choir (sometimes), and the priest and other ministers who may be participating. The first part of the service, the Liturgy of the Word, includes the reading of Bible passages, a homily, recitation of "the creed," and prayers. The Eucharistic Liturgy is the administering of Holy Communion. Hymns are sung and music played at various times throughout the service. Near the end of the communion rite of the mass, the priest will invite parishioners to offer and exchange signs of peace—customarily exchanging a handshake and "peace be with you"– with persons nearby and to greet guests. The congregation rises for the processionals.

❖ **Marriage Ceremonies:** The Catholic wedding ceremony usually takes place in the main sanctuary of the church or in a smaller chapel and frequently includes a Mass. The priest is the officiant. Some wedding couples provide a wedding ceremony program to help guests understand and participate more easily. Because the Roman Catholic Church does not allow secular music, some Catholic churches do not allow the classic wedding march or recessional.

❖ **Mourning and Funerals:** For a Catholic funeral, mourners can send flowers to the home of the deceased's family, the funeral home, or the church, being sure to indicate that the flowers are to be used for the funeral service. If the family requests charitable donations in lieu of flowers, honor that request. The respectful non-Catholic can also give the deceased family a mass card. In return for a donation to the Church; the Church will say prayers or mass on behalf of the deceased's soul.

As the model for Catholic funerals is the Easter journey of Jesus Christ, the funeral is generally celebrated in three stages—prayer vigil (wake), funeral liturgy, and committal.

A wake, which gives the family sympathy and support in their grief, is usually held in the days before the actual funeral service. Whether held at a funeral parlor or in someone's home, guests are expected to sign a register. If the casket is present, quietly stand by it praying or thinking about the deceased before mingling with others. Guests who are not close to family members should introduce themselves and tell them how they knew the deceased.

The liturgy, usually celebrated in the church, is the main celebration for the deceased person. Most Roman Catholic funerals are also requiem (funeral) Masses; however, some celebrations do not include a Mass.

Mourners should all be seated before the family arrives to be seated in the reserved front pews. At end of the service, the coffin will be carried out of the church with family immediately following.

The committal, the final act of leave-taking, takes place at the graveside or crematorium. (In 1963, Pope Paul VI revoked the canon forbidding cremation.) At the end of a graveside service, the priest will invite mourners to make a gesture of farewell—sprinkling holy water, leaving a special flower, or sprinkling earth over the gravesite. At the end of a crematorium service, the coffin will disappear behind a screen or curtain.

Funerals are usually followed by a reception at a family home or other nearby location. Most mourners attend.

Memorial services or services of thanksgiving that celebrate the life of the deceased may be held later. Some Catholic churches have an annual special Mass near the end of the year to celebrate all those who have died during the previous year.

❖ **Meeting the Pope (Pontiff):** Dress appropriately—a tuxedo or dark suit, tie, and polished shoes for a man and a black or dark dress or suit that covers the shoulders, chest, arms, and knees for a woman. Only in private hearings are women required to cover their heads, usually with black veiling. Jewelry and accessories should be elegant and subdued. Do not wear gloves. The privilege of wearing a white dress during a hearing is granted only to Catholic queens or Catholic spouses of kings.

All visits follow a protocol, are highly organized, and are accompanied by high security. Comply with all instructions concerning where to stand and sit and how to behave in the audience room. When the Pope enters a room, stand and applaud.

If the Pope approaches you, genuflect (go down on one knee or make a low bow). If he offers his hand and you are not Catholic, you may shake it. If you are Catholic, you may kiss his ring on right hand. Kissing his ring is meant as a sign of affection and respect. When the Pope prepares to leave an event, stand and wait for him to leave the room before doing anything else.

If you receive a private or semiprivate audience, be prepared to speak with the pontiff. He will probably offer a small gift of religious nature. You are not expected to bring a gift unless you are a head of state!

DRESS

Dress modestly and appropriately for basic service and Mass as well as for special occasions. Men are usually expected to wear a coat and tie. Dark colors are appropriate for funerals. Women do not need to cover their heads.

PARTICIPATION

Guests of other faiths are not expected to use the holy water fonts, make the sign of the cross, or genuflect, but they ARE expected to sit and stand with the congregation. Kneeling, reading aloud, and singing are optional. Do not receive communion or say any prayers contradictory to your own faith and beliefs. Guests may, however, join others at the altar rail to receive a blessing—placing your hands across your chest indicates this desire. Guests may contribute to the offering.

WHAT NOT TO DO

- ❖ Bring food or drink into the church.
- ❖ Chew gum.
- ❖ Read the church bulletin during Mass.

❖ Receive from the chalice if you are ill.

❖ Leave before the end of the recession.

❖ Wear a hat or cap if you are a man.

LEXICON

CHALICE: Receptacle that holds the wine consecrated for the Communion service. It is coated inside with gold

CONFESSIONAL: A specially divided booth in which the priest can hear what is said by the confessor sitting on the other side.

GENUFLECT: To bend the right knee with hands held in front of chest in reverence to the altar and to the cross

HOLY EUCHARIST: Also called Holy Communion, this sacrament of sharing bread (Christ's body) and wine (Christ's blood) relates to the Last Supper Jesus had with his disciples and represents remembrance of him.

HOLY ROSARY: A string of beads used to count a sequence of prayers. It usually consists of a crucifix (cross) and five sections of ten beads each (decades). Each decade is separated by single beads and meditation on one of the Mysteries of the Rosary, which recall the life of Jesus.

HOLY WATER FONTS: Receptacles at a church's entrance contain holy water for Roman Catholics to use when entering. They dip their first two fingers into the font, and then use them to make the sign of the cross: they tap their foreheads, center of their chests, and each shoulder.

HOMILY: Sermon.

PATEN: Shallow metal dish or tray that holds the Communion bread.

STATIONS OF THE CROSS: Usually around the walls of a Catholic church, you will find fourteen different pictures or carvings depicting Christ's journey from condemnation to crucifixion to tomb.

HINDU

If I were asked to define the Hindu creed, I should simply say search after truth through nonviolent means. A man may not believe in God and still call himself a Hindu. Hinduism is a relentless pursuit after truth…Hinduism is the religion of truth.

                           –Mahatma Gandhi

H*induism teaches that God is within and transcends all beings and objects, that the purpose of life to become aware of our divine essence, and that different forms of worship through images and rituals are helpful to different persons. Unlike most other religions, Hinduism has no founder or common creed. A place for community worship and reverence, the Hindu temple and its rituals are designed to inspire visitors, helping them to realize a higher state of mind. Observing proper etiquette and respect for rituals helps to preserve the aura of peace conducive to worship. The guest is expected to sit cross-legged on the floor quietly during the meditations, chanting, and readings from sacred texts.*

SERVICES AND CEREMONIES

- ❖ **Basic Service**: Because Hindu temples (*mandir*) are considered the residences of particular gods or goddesses, in the center of the temple is a small room or area containing images of those deities. Most Hindus make a sign of reverence by touching their hand to the ground and then touching their forehead with that hand, symbolizing the placing of temple sand on their foreheads. They fold their hands as gesture of respect. They may signal their arrival by ringing the temple bell at the entrance.

Guests are expected to remove shoes before entering the sanctuary and place them with the others. Enter with clean feet: many temples have taps outside for washing the feet. Some temples do not allow devotees to bring items of leather into the temple. There will be a tap nearby for washing your hands before entering. When sitting, do not extend your feet toward the religious leader or toward an altar.

After entering, devotees will pay respect to the main deity and may receive a blessing of red powder on their foreheads from the priest.

❖ **Marriage Ceremonies**: Held after sunset and before sunrise, Hindu weddings are considered a sacrament and are rich with symbolic meaning. Although traditional Indian weddings frequently extend over many weeks, the several celebrations are now likely to be consolidated into one or two weeks. The day before the wedding, family and good friends gather at each partner's home to pray and eat. In the evening there are separate parties for the bride and groom with music, dancing, and feasting. The bride will have her hands and feet painted with henna with intricate *mehndi* designs. Her female friends and family will also have their hands painted.

If the wedding is held in a temple, women should keep their upper arms, legs, and chests covered. Otherwise, wear whatever you would normally wear to such a festive occasion. Women are always welcome to wear saris. Traditional Indian foods are served both before and after the ceremony. It is considered impolite to refuse to eat or drink. Gifts of household goods brought to the ceremony may be placed in a designated area.

The wedding itself is both elaborate and lengthy and can take place in any covered area—a special room of a temple, hotel, home, catering hall, or outside (covered with tent or canopy). Ceremonies take place under a four-pillared canopy (*mandap*), which is covered with draped fabric and decorated with flowers and lights. When entering, the groom may stomp on a clay pot to demonstrate that he has the strength, ability, and fortitude to overcome any obstacles that the couple may face in the future. Escorted by her parents, the bride then joins him for blessings. A guest program is seldom distributed.

There are seven wedding ceremonies: the verbal contract between parents or guardians; the giving away of the bride by her father or guardian; the welcoming of the bride and groom; the ceremonious holding of each other's hands by the bride and groom; lighting the sacred fire which the couple ritualistically encircle; and the groom's painting his and his bride's forehead in red.

❖ **Mourning and Funerals:** The cremation sacrament is the most important and sacred of all rituals. There is a twelve- to thirty-day period of mourning during which mourners dress, behave, and eat austerely. Inside the home, a lamp remains lit, incense is burned, mirrors may be covered, and religious pictures may be turned to the wall. At the end of the mourning period, the house is thoroughly cleaned.

Hindu funerals usually take place within twenty-four hours after a person's death, because the soul needs to begin its next journey as soon as possible to avoid becoming a ghost, or a soul without a home. The body remains at home until taken to the place of cremation. If initially taken to a funeral parlor, the body will be brought back home so that the family can perform various rites of washing, blessing, and chanting. It is appropriate to send cards of sympathy and bring flowers to the home of the deceased where they are usually placed at the person's feet. Donations are not customary.

If you are invited to the crematorium, stay in the waiting area until the funeral procession has passed and then follow. Guests at the crematorium are expected to view the body and then sit through the service. A last food offering is symbolically made to the deceased prior to cremation.

At some point in the rituals, a priest will perform the final good-bye. The *sapindikarana* ritual is the cutting of a dough-like substance in half and then dividing one half into three parts. The remaining half represents the deceased, and the other three parts are his previous three generations. The priest blends all four pieces together to signify that the deceased has now become an ancestor.

A post-funeral gathering is held at the home of the deceased or other local venue. As an act of ritual purification, the chief mourner will sprinkle guests with water before they enter.

You may be invited to a *shraddha,* which occurs ten to thirty days after death. This ceremony, which liberates the soul of the deceased so that it can ascend to heaven, is performed at home. Visitors to the home during the mourning period are expected to bring fruit.

❖ **Other Important Hindu Life-Cycle Events, Holy Days and Festivals:**

> o **Naming and Rice-Eating Ceremonies:** When a child is twelve days old, guests may be invited to a formal naming. In the West, however, this ritual is frequently later combined with other ceremonies, including a rice-eating ceremony, which marks the first time the child eats solid food. The event usually takes place at the child's home, and gifts for the child are expected.

> o **Diwali:** The Festival of Lights, which takes place over a five-day period, is frequently likened to the Christian celebration of Christmas. Hindus send Diwali cards, exchange gifts, prepare a feast, and set off fireworks displays. If you are invited to a Hindu home for a celebratory meal, remove your shoes and greet older persons with the traditional *namaste* bow. If flatware is not provided, use the flat bread (*chapati*) to scoop up your food or push food into small bundles to pick up with your right hand. Do not bring a gift of wine or liquor unless you are certain that your host will welcome alcohol.

> o Because the Hindu calendar is lunar based, specific dates of Hindu holidays vary from year to year. Other

important holidays include: Krishna Janmashtami, the birthday celebration of Krishna, and Holi–Dhuleti, a festival of colors commemorating the triumph of good over evil and celebrating the beginning of spring.

DRESS

Short or tight skirts do not lend themselves to sitting cross-legged on the floor. Wear shoes that can be easily removed. Although temples vary, conservative clothing is always acceptable. Women should keep their upper arms, chests, and legs covered when visiting a temple. No head coverings are required. There are no restrictions on the color of clothing.

PARTICIPATION

"Namaste" is an appropriate Hindu greeting and parting. It is spoken with a slight bow and your hands at chest level, pressed together with palms touching and fingers pointing upward. Remain silent throughout any ceremony except during chanting. Some temples encourage your participation by providing copies of popular slokas in English. All pujas and rituals follow set procedures. Try not to do anything that would distract devotees who are participating in these rituals in front of various shrines throughout the temple.

WHAT NOT TO DO

❖ Wear footwear or shorts into the temple.

❖ Bring any non-vegetarian foods (including egg), mushrooms, onion, or garlic into the temple or its kitchen.

❖ If you are a woman, offer to shake hands with a Buddhist monk. Monks wearing the bright orange robes of an ascetic often avoid contact with women altogether as part of their practice of strict self-denial.

LEXICON

ASHRAM: A place for spiritual retreat.

BHAKTI: Devotion and submission to the Lord.

DARSHAN: Means "sight" or "seeing." An auspicious viewing of a deity whereby the viewer can receive a blessing.

GURU: A spiritual teacher.

MANDIR: A Hindu temple that has been designed or adapted according to special guidelines.

MANTRA: Repetition of sacred Sanskrit sounds/prayers.

MURTI: A statue of a deity.

PANDIT: A scholar of sacred texts.

PUJA: An offering or gift to deities or distinguished persons.

PRASAD: Sacramental food.

SATSANG: Collective prayer.

SLOKA: Prayerful verse.

SWAMI: A Hindu monk.

Islamic

*No man is a true believer unless he desires for his brother
that which he desires for himself.*

–Sayings of The Prophet

Islam is based on the sayings and teachings of the Prophet Mohammed
that are written in the Quran. A true Muslim is defined as "someone who lives in peace" by surrendering to the will of Allah. Although
most Muslims are Sunni, others are Shi'ites, and there are wide-ranging
national and cultural differences. Muslims believe that all have equal
access to Allah, and there are no ordained priests, officiants, or ministers.

SERVICES AND CEREMONIES

❖ **Basic Service:** Although Muslims pray five times each day, it
   need not be in a mosque. On Friday, however, the noon or
   early afternoon prayer is recited at a central mosque, and
   the program includes a sermon. To purify oneself before
   standing in front of Allah, Muslims use special facilities to
   wash their hands, faces, and feet with water. To pray, the
   congregation stands behind the imam, facing Mecca. Each
   gender has its own prayer line or area, or there is a separate balcony for women only. Worshipers stand, bow, and

prostrate themselves in unison. If there is no special room for women, they pray behind the men. All seating is on the floor. Muslims pray and listen to the Quran with their palms facing upward.

Non-Muslim visitors are invited to sit to the back or side as observers. There are no refreshments after the service; however, worshipers may stay after the Friday service to further read and discuss the Quran.

❖ **Marriage Ceremonies:** Marriage, the foundation of Muslim society, is considered a sacred contract, not a sacrament. The ceremony for the signing of the marriage contract (*nikah*) is sometimes attended by only members of the immediate family. This is followed by a wedding feast (*walima*) at a later time or date. Westernized modern customs combine a ceremony and reception, with the reception held in a home, mosque, or catering establishment immediately after the ceremony. If the reception is held in a mosque, there is no music or dancing. Some Middle Eastern *walimas* are segregated, male and female, with each group having its own celebration.

Women must wear head covering in mosques, dress modestly, and should wear clothing in which they can comfortably sit cross-legged on the floor. Remove shoes when entering a prayer area. Gifts may be sent to the newlyweds' home or brought to the ceremony.

❖ **Mourning and Funerals:** Specific funeral rites vary by region and interpretation. In most Islamic cultures, after ritually washing and enshrouding the body, the community offers collective prayers for the forgiveness of the dead. The body (which is not embalmed) is buried as quickly as possible and, when permitted, without a casket. The Muslim funeral takes place in a funeral home or in a room of the mosque. Although not necessary for guests, Muslims wear black.

The imam presides over the funeral prayers while attendees face Mecca in three rows: men, children, and women. In some Islamic cultures, only the men may attend the actual interment. After the burial, Muslim mourners may wait by the graveside while the deceased is being questioned by angels. Cremation is not permitted. After the funeral, the Muslim community may prepare food for mourners and their guests.

Although religiously mandated not to exceed forty days, the period of mourning is usually three days. Some widows traditionally observe *iddat,* a period of four months and ten days during which they cannot wear bright or decorative clothing or jewelry, change residences, leave home except for work or errands, and cannot remarry. Muslims do not customarily mark their graves with headstones.

Local custom varies concerning the bringing or sending of flowers. Food may be brought to the mourners' home during the initial period of mourning.

❖ **Other Important Muslim Life Cycle Events and Holy Days**

   o **Birth:** Although Muslims do not traditionally celebrate birthdays, modern Muslims often send and receive cards of congratulations upon the birth of a child.

   o **The Feast of Ramadan:** This holiday (held in the ninth month of the lunar year) celebrates the breaking of a thirty-day fast. From sunrise to sunset, Muslims abstain from food, drink, smoking, and sexual activity. During this period Muslims also reflect, express gratitude, atone for past sins, and perform acts of charity and kindness. At the end of the fast, family and community members gather for three days to feast, attend mosque, exchange presents, and give alms to the poor. The thoughtful friend, neighbor, or coworker will greet the faster with "Ramadan Mubarak"—May God give you a blessed month!—or even "Happy Ramadan" and will remember not to schedule an important business lunch during this period. Feast guests are expected to eat heartily and enjoy.

DRESS

Before entering a mosque—and most Muslim homes—remove your shoes. Socks are acceptable. Women's clothing should be conservative and include a skirt. Arms and chests should be covered and hems should reach below the knees. Women must wear a scarf over their heads; men do not wear a head covering.

PARTICIPATION

Non-Muslims do not participate in any of the prayers or rituals.

WHAT NOT TO DO

❖ Eat or drink (even water) in the presence of those who are fasting during the month of Ramadan.

❖ Take photos of Muslims without receiving their permission first.

- ❖ Wear jewelry with faces or heads of animals, signs of the zodiac, Stars of David, or crosses in a mosque or to any Muslim ritual or celebration.

- ❖ Smoke in the vicinity of a mosque.

- ❖ When attending a service as a guest, do not make a contribution or donation to the mosque, as it would be violating the generosity and hospitality Muslims typically exhibit toward guests.

- ❖ Perform *raka'ah* or prayer if you are a non-Muslim.

- ❖ Leave a service while congregational prayer is being conducted.

- ❖ Wail or weep loudly at funerals, as the deceased's spirit may hear and become anguished.

LEXICON

HAJJ: The pilgrimage to Mecca.

IMAM: Officiant who provides guidance, leads prayers, and delivers sermons.

MECCA: A city in western Saudi Arabia that is the birthplace of Mohammed and the spiritual center of Islam. Muslims always face toward Mecca during prayers.

MIHRAB: A curved niche in the wall of a mosque that indicates the direction of Mecca.

MUSALLAH: The prayer room in a mosque; there may be separate areas for men and women.

RAKA'AH: Part of a prayer ritual that includes motions and recitations.

WADU: Washings of hands, faces, and feet with water.

JEWISH

*Judaism is a religion of time, aiming at the sanctification
of time... the Sabbaths are our great cathedrals.*
    −Rabbi Abraham Joshua Heschel, *The Sabbath*

Judaism, a monotheistic religion, has different branches, sects, and traditions. Jews sanctify their lives through prayer, education, and observance of the ethical precepts of the Torah—the Five Books of Moses. The main historical division is between the Sephardim and Ashkenazim, originating in medieval Spain and Germany, respectively. There are no major doctrinal differences, but each differs in culture, traditions, rituals, and liturgical practices.*

The main branches of Judaism in the West are Orthodox, Conservative, Reconstructionist and Reform; within each of these, there are several approaches. Theologically, Reform Judaism is the most liberal; Orthodox Judaism, the most traditional, also includes several fundamentalist groups such as the Hasidim.

SERVICES AND CEREMONIES

❖ **Basic Service:** Hebrew, the traditional language of Jewish worship, is used in services and celebrations of all Jewish religious movements. Each service contains many common elements with minor variations relating to the time of day and month. In Orthodox synagogues, men and women sit separately (there is sometimes a women's gallery above). Reform congregations sit together.

The Jewish calendar day does not begin at midnight, but at sunset or when three medium-sized stars should be visible. The basic services take place on Friday evening and Saturday morning of the Jewish Sabbath (Shabbat), which begins at eighteen minutes before sunset on Friday and ends at nightfall on Saturday. The service has well-defined sections, which open with blessings and passages being read to a standing congregation and include silent recitation, a series of praises and petitions to God, and a public reading from the Torah scroll. The period of silent mediation takes place standing with feet together facing the direction of the Temple in Jerusalem. The congregation also stands for the opening of the Ark and the procession carrying the Torah. Then they are seated for its reading. The Saturday service is more extensive than the Friday evening service; and Orthodox and Conservative services are usually longer than those of Reform or Reconstructionist congregations.

Following the service, the congregation socializes with a communal *kiddush*, sanctifying the Shabbat with wine or grape juice and refreshments of challah bread, cakes, crackers, gefilte fish, and cheese blintzes. Guests are not expected to taste the wine.

If you are invited to a Jewish home during Shabbat, some or all of the following may be observed: special meals, such as the Friday evening Shabbat meal; abstinence from all work, including cooking, carrying, driving, viewing television, etc.; food and food preparation according to Jewish dietary laws (kosher), including the separate storage, preparation, and eating of meat and dairy products; reading or discussion of some aspect of the Torah; and putting away objects considered forbidden (*muktzah,* or "needing to be set aside") during Shabbat, including phones, tablets, money, magazines, and notebooks. Male guests may be offered a *kippah,* or *yarmulke,* to wear.

In following these ancient traditions and rituals, take your lead from your host and the other people present—and enjoy. The usual greeting is "Shabbat shalom" (Peaceful Sabbath).

❖ **Marriage Ceremonies:** A Jewish marriage is a sacred bond and a joyful occasion. On the wedding morning, it is customary for the bride to host a meal for close female guests and for the groom to do the same for his male guests.

The wedding ceremony itself takes place under a canopy (*huppah*), which is supported by four poles, and symbolizes the canopy of the heavens and the home they will first share together. The ceremony usually begins with a blessing and a shared cup of wine by the bride and groom as a sign of rejoicing. At the conclusion of the wedding ceremony, the groom crushes a (wrapped) glass with his foot. There are numerous interpretations of this custom—such as symbolic of the fragility of a relationship or as a reminder of the destruction of the Temple in Jerusalem.

The wedding feast is held in a reception room of the synagogue/temple, a wedding hall, hotel, or other venue, or outside. There is great celebration with music, dancing, and food. Wait for a blessing to be said before eating or drinking. The traditional greeting for the family is "Mazel tov" (Congratulations).

Kippah/yarmulke are provided for male guests who are expected to dress in keeping with the formality of the event. Women's attire also depends on the formality of the wedding; for most women, this is an occasion for festive dress.

A generous wedding gift is a Jewish custom, and usually gifts can be selected and sent from a bridal registry. A gift of money is appropriate. However, if mailing a gift certificate, check, or bond before the wedding, it should be made out to the bride-to-be and sent to her home. If presented at the wedding reception or later, it should be made out to both the bride and groom,

❖ **Mourning and Funerals:** Jews are buried in consecrated burial grounds twenty-four hours after death, if possible. Traditional Jewish law forbids cremation; however, cremation is allowed among some Reform Jews.

The funeral ceremony may take place at a temple/synagogue or at a funeral home. There will not be an open casket. The service, which is conducted by the rabbi, includes prayers, eulogies, and music. Sometimes only family and close friends attend the interment. Once mourners have arrived at a traditional burial service, there is a processional to the grave itself. At the gravesite, prayers are recited. Non-Jews may participate in filling in the grave at the end of the service.

After the burial, guests are invited to the home of the bereaved, who will be in intense mourning (*shiva*) for seven days. The bereaved sit on low stools to receive visitors. Do not plan to stay long or bring gifts or flowers. Offer condolences to each mourner, and do not sit unless the bereaved are seated. If you bring food—even if some of the family members are not ritually observant—be sure the food is kosher.

While the bereaved sit *shiva*, prayers are held each morning and evening except during Shabbat. A seven-day memorial candle is kept burning, and mirrors are covered. In a traditional house of mourning, one does not greet the mourner.

One is considered a mourner for twelve months for a parent and thirty days for other relatives. Although the thirty-day period of mourning is less intense, there are still many restrictions, especially for the Orthodox mourner who cannot leave the house for seven days. Among the restricted activities are: shaving, getting a haircut, or cutting one's nails; listening to music or attending social events; and any activities that are not in the spirit of mourning.

It is customary to call or visit the bereaved at home and/ or send a card or letter of condolence. Flowers, considered reminders of worldly pleasures or vanity, are not acceptable for Orthodox, Conservative, or Reconstructionist funerals but are sometimes appropriate for Reform funerals. It is customary to make a charitable contribution in the name of the deceased to a cause supported by the deceased or the deceased's family. Because the Hebrew number for eighteen spells the word *chai*, meaning "life," memorial donations are often made in amounts that are multiples of eighteen.

❖ **Other Important Jewish Life-Cycle Events and Holy Days:** Jewish tradition has many holidays and celebrations. From

Bat/Bas Mitzvahs and Rosh Hashanah to housewarmings and Passover, traditions and etiquette are a significant and symbolic part of their enriching history.

    o **Passover/Pesach Seder**: If you are fortunate enough to be invited to a Seder, you will experience the home holiday most widely observed even by those who no longer participate formally in the other aspects of Jewish worship. The keynote of Jewish identity, this festival of freedom is rich in symbolism and is family-centered. Passover celebrates God's guidance and protection that helped Moses to lead the Jewish people to freedom from slavery in Egypt. The ritual seder meal, which commences the festival, is a family gathering, and traditionally includes special friends and those who are far from their own homes. The recitation of the Haggadah—the story of the exodus from Egypt—and traditional readings, questions, prayers, and songs are both traditional and symbolic. The meal itself is historically rooted: foods and wines, each representing some aspect of the Passover story, are shared in a specific order. At some tables, families will place an empty chair and a full glass of wine for Elijah, the precursor of the Messiah.

The Seder guest has several obligations: to be prompt, to eat some matzo, to partake of each of the four cups of wine or grape juice at the Seder, and to try to participate in the reading and singing. It is usual for the Seder guest to bring a gift for the family. To avoid embarrassment, a non-food gift is probably the simpler choice, as standards of observance regarding food vary.

o **Birth Ceremony:** The Brit, or naming ceremony, is used for both newborn males and females. For a male child, the Brit Milah occurs on the eighth day of his life and centers around his circumcision. This may be performed at home, in a synagogue/temple, or in a hospital. At this time, the child also receives his Hebrew name and is given godparents. For girls, the Brit Bat can also be held at home but often takes place in a temple/synagogue on the first Shabbat after their birth. The baby is dressed in white. A small party or reception is customarily held after each of these ceremonies, and the invited guests usually bring gifts. Whether attending one of these events or receiving a birth announcement, one may wish to send or bring a gift. Note that there is a strong tradition of reluctance to prepare too much in advance before the birth of a Jewish child, thus most gifts are given after the child is born and the name announced.

Instead of practicing circumcision, some Reform Jews have a welcoming ceremony for male babies called Brit Shalom (Covenant of Peace).

o **Bar Mitzvah/Bat Mitzvah:** These ceremonies for Jewish thirteen-year-olds, which celebrate the age of religious adulthood and responsibility, are a combination of public event and social occasion. Invitations are usually sent far in advance. Some synagogues/temples have a Bat Chayil (Daughter of Valour) ceremony for a group of thirteen-year-old girls who have completed a prescribed study course. The service, which is usually for family and invited guests, includes prayers, readings, and presentations by the girls. It also may be followed by a reception or special celebration.

The Bar (for boys) or Bat (for girls) Mitzvah service is always part of a larger temple/synagogue service and frequently takes place on a Saturday morning. Guests at Reform or Reconstructionist services are expected to arrive at the beginning of the service; guests at Conservative or Orthodox services may be told that they can arrive at the specific event time within the longer service. Do not enter when the congregation is standing or during the rabbi's sermon.

On this occasion, the young person, for the first time, reads aloud from the Torah or the Haftarah and may deliver a speech about the significance of the occasion.

Lasting gifts are most appropriate for this occasion. Customary Bar/Bat Mitzvah gifts are cash, bonds, significant religious jewelry, or ritual items of Judaica. Israeli art objects or coins made into medallions, a donation to a charity in the youth's name, trees planted in Israel, a biography of a Jewish hero or heroine, or music by Jewish composers would also be suitable. Because Orthodox Jews do not carry objects during Shabbat, you should not bring a gift to a synagogue unless you are certain that carrying is acceptable. You can send the gift to the youth's home before or after the ceremony.

After the ceremony, there is usually a brief reception (*kiddush*) for the entire congregation and guests. For invited guests there may be a special celebration later with a full meal, music, dancing, and speeches at a home, reception room of synagogue/temple, or other venue.

o **Rosh Hashanah (Jewish New Year):** It is thoughtful to remember Jewish friends, colleagues, or relatives at Rosh Hashanah by sending greeting cards. If the recipient is a business acquaintance, you may send the card to the office. Cards are usually sent out about ten days before the September holiday. Because the Hebrew letters of the word "nuts" can also form an acrostic spelling "sin," some avoid giving nuts for Jewish religious celebrations.

o **Hanukkah, the Festival of Lights**: Hanukkah is celebrated by the lighting of the special menorah on each of the eight nights of the December holiday. A Hanukkah party guest may bring almost any type of gift for the host, although Jewish items are especially appropriate.

DRESS

When in synagogue/temple, all men cover their heads. If you are a man and have no head covering, you will be given a skullcap (kippah/yarmulke) to wear. Although informal attire is permitted in more liberal congregations, *a jacket and tie is always appropriate. Women's clothing should be modest, influenced by local custom and fashion. If you are a married woman, you must wear a head covering during an Orthodox or more conservative service. In Orthodox congregations, women's clothing should cover chest and arms and hems should cover the knees. Although the Jewish men will be wearing a tallit (striped, tasseled prayer shawl), non-Jewish men should not wear them.*

Since Jewish law prohibits labor, including the carrying of objects, on Shabbat, do not carry bags or purses into an Orthodox synagogue for Sabbath services.

PARTICIPATION

Guests who are not Jewish are expected to stand with the congregation. Reading and singing are optional.

WHAT NOT TO DO

- ❖ Openly wear symbols of another faith, such as a cross.

- ❖ Turn your back on the Torah when it passes you or remain seated while the Ark is open.

- ❖ Place prayer books on the floor, as they contain God's name and should not be disrespected.

- ❖ Bring gifts to a wedding ceremony. Gifts are appropriate at the reception..

LEXICON

ARK: Cabinet on the pulpit where the Torah is kept.

CANTOR: One who sings or chants part of the service and leads the congregation in song.

MAZAL TOV: Means congratulations (literally "good luck").

MENORAH: Seven-branched candelabra that was part of the ancient Temple in Jerusalem.

MINYAN: A quorum of at least ten persons over the age of thirteen required for communal prayer.

RABBI: One who leads the services, teaches and preaches.

SIDDUR: Prayer book.

Protestant

*I cannot choose but adhere to the word of God, which has
possession of my conscience, nor can I possibly, nor will
I ever, make any recantation since it is neither safe nor
honest to act contrary to conscience.*

— Martin Luther

The Protestant tradition encompasses a wide variety of ministries,
including Episcopal, Lutheran, Reformed, Methodist, Mormon,
Baptist, Congregational, Presbyterian, Society of Friends, Amish, and
Jehovah's Witnesses. These ministries include very diverse social, racial,
and ethnic groups.

Protestant theologies may be conservative, moderate, or liberal, and each
denomination has different branches, beliefs, and rituals. However, there
are many shared practices and traditions, such as Sunday services and
celebrations of Christ's birth and resurrection on Christmas and Easter,
respectively. Contemporary sacraments of Holy Communion/the Lord's
Supper and baptism vary greatly in their rituals. For example, baptism
can be performed for an infant or an adult, with sprinkled water or immer-
sion; the Lord's Supper can be offered to all or restricted to those baptized
in a particular faith and can include the serving of wine or grape juice or
leavened or unleavened bread.

Some rituals, such as the altar call (Evangelical), speaking in tongues (Pentecostal), and spirit-led worship (Quaker) are particularly distinctive.

SERVICES AND CEREMONIES

❖ **Basic Service:** Although they will vary greatly, most Protestant Sunday morning services include prayers, Bible readings, responsive readings, singing of hymns/psalms by a choir and the congregation, the preaching of God's word (sermon) from the pastor, a voluntary offering, and, often, the communion liturgy. Most Protestant services last about an hour, although some Evangelical services can last much longer. After the service, it is customary for the pastor/officiant to stand at the rear of the church and thank the congregation and guests for coming—and for those attending to thank the pastor for the service.

Many Protestant churches will have Bible classes or Sunday School prior to or concurrent with (for young chidren) the regular Sunday morning service as well as a Sunday evening worship service and a Bible class or prayer meeting service on Wednesday evenings.

❖ **Marriage Ceremonies:** The Protestant marriage ceremony is usually a ceremony in itself but—especially in the Episcopal/Anglican Church—can be part of a Holy Communion service. The Protestant wedding can take place in the church, a home, out-of-doors, a wedding hall, a restaurant, or any other setting of the couple's choice. Usually the pastor or priest presides, sometimes with another officiant who represents the different faith of one of the marriage partners. Both music and wedding vows may be traditional or specific to the desires or interests of the couple.

❖ **Mourning and Funerals:** Protestant funerals usually take place within a week after death in the church or in a funeral parlor; most are burials, but some are cremations. If you are unfamiliar with the rituals of a certain faith, it is best to check with family members, the church, or the funeral parlor to learn whether there will be a wake, if flowers would be appropriate, where to send contributions, and/or to ask for directions to the cemetery. There is usually a reception following the interment or cremation.

DRESS

As with Protestant rituals, dress codes vary depending on fashion and locale. Protestant churches do not have any rules concerning head coverings, jewelry, removal of footwear, covering of arms, and length of skirt or colors. Jackets and ties are always appropriate for men, but more casual clothing is the norm in some cultures. In general, clothing is expected to be modest. Pants or pantsuits for women are usually acceptable.

PARTICIPATION

Guests are welcome to participate in almost any aspects of the service that they feel comfortable with. It is not necessary to stand, sit, or kneel with the congregation, but it is respectful. As noted previously, some churches restrict participation in the Last Supper to those baptized in that faith.

WHAT NOT TO DO

❖ If you are not of the faith, do not partake of Holy Communion unless the church permits it—and many do.

❖ Wear shorts to a service or ceremony.

❖ Enter church during the spoken part of the service.

❖ Exit the church while prayers are being recited or while a sermon or homily is being delivered.

LEXICON

ALTAR CALL: An invitation to come forward after the sermon to make a spiritual commitment.

BAPTISTRY/BAPTISMAL FONT: Area of church used for baptizing or christening. It can be a font, bowl, or pool.

EUCHARIST/HOLY COMMUNION/THE LAST SUPPER: The last meal Jesus Christ shared with his disciples.

GOSPEL: As used during a worship service, this refers to a New Testament reading from writings of Jesus' life by four of his apostles.

HOMILY: Sermon or discourse on a practical matter or of a moral theme.

Mormon (The Church of Latter Day Saints)

True independence and freedom can only exist in doing what is right.

–Brigham Young

Considered by some to be a part of the Protestant movement, many Mormon beliefs are similar to those of orthodox Christians. They celebrate both Christmas and Easter. They use the King James version of the Bible as well as the Book of Mormon and its related publications. However, even Protestant guests may require some additional information before attending a religious ceremony.

Worship services are conducted in local churches/church houses and in temples, which are dedicated to God and used for special worship and ceremonies for both the living and for dead ancestors. Churches are local, whereas temples may be located at some distance from members. Guests are not welcome in a temple, as only faithful (recommended) members of the Church of Latter Day Saints (LDS) may enter.

There is no professional clergy, and churches are led and staffed by lay members who receive no financial compensation. The LDS also has thousands of young missionaries throughout the world who serve for two years at their own expense.

If you will be entertaining or serving Mormons, be aware of their dietary restrictions, which include coffee, tea, alcohol, and, sometimes, soda. Herbal tisanes are a good alternative to tea and coffee. Members are encouraged to fast one day each month, donating to charity the amount they would have spent on food.

SERVICES AND CEREMONIES

❖ **Basic Service**: The Sunday service is called a "sacrament meeting," and the chief officiant is referred to as "Bishop" followed by his last name. The service usually lasts about an hour and includes song, an opening prayer, communion with sacramental prayers, talks/sermon, and a benediction. Youths from the congregation play an important part in the service. The congregation stands midway through the service during the singing of the "Rest Hymn". It is one's personal choice whether to receive the sacrament/communion.

❖ **Marriage Ceremonies:** Most often, LDS ceremonies are small and intimate, and guests receive invitations for the ring ceremony and/or reception only. However, guests may be invited to a church or elsewhere for a civil wedding ceremony or to a temple for a sealing ceremony. Often, the civil ceremony is followed months—or even years—later by the temple sealing ceremony that binds the union for eternity.

The civil ceremony is usually conducted in the cultural hall of the church house, with music, decorations, and vows similar to those of most Protestant churches. However, no candles or dehydrated materials are allowed. A reception or open house usually follows at the church or at another location, and guests are free to come and go as they please.

The temple wedding itself is quite short and is usually limited to immediate family and a few close friends. Temples provide guests who do not have a "temple recommend" with waiting rooms, visitor centers, and tranquil grounds.

Gifts are usually taken to the postnuptial reception.

❖ **Mourning and Funerals:** The Mormon funeral typically takes place within one week after the death. Family members and very close friends may be invited to attend a special prayer service before the funeral. The ceremony is held in a church, at a funeral home and/or at the graveside. Caskets are not usually left open during the service. The sixty- to ninety-minute service itself will include music, prayer, and eulogies. Guests may also attend the interment where a family member dedicates the grave with a prayer.

After the service, it is appropriate to visit the home of the bereaved where light food may be served.

Unless otherwise informed, flowers may be sent before or after the funeral either to the funeral home or to the home of the bereaved. Contributions may be sent to a charity of the deceased's choice. There are no rituals for observing the anniversary of a death.

❖ **Family Home Evening:** Although it is unusual that guests would be invited to this weekly event, friends should be aware that Mormon families usually observe a home evening with family on Monday nights (although it may be held on another day). The purpose is to strengthen family ties through singing, praying, reading, walking, game playing, etc.

DRESS

Dignified and modest clothing is expected for both men and women. Men usually wear a suit or sport jacket. No head coverings are required, and all colors are acceptable.

PARTICIPATION

Guests attending a Latter Day Saints' meeting, service, or ceremony are not expected to participate, although they may sing and pray with the congregation if it does not conflict with their own religious beliefs.

WHAT NOT TO DO

❖ Photograph, film, or audio-record in a church or temple.

❖ Wear revealing or "flashy" clothing to church or temple.

❖ Enter or leave a service during communion.

LEXICON

THE BOOK OF MORMON: The revelations from God published in 1830 by Joseph Smith. In addition to his earlier visions of God and Jesus Christ, he was visited by the angel Moroni who told him the location of the golden tablets containing the teachings.

BROTHER AND SISTER: Terms used to address or refer to fellow church members.

ELDERS: An elevated office within the Melchizedek Priesthood whose male members can lead meetings, baptize, bless, administer to other members, etc.

THE WORD OF WISDOM: The divinely revealed health code that forbids the use of tobacco, alcoholic beverages, tea, and coffee and emphasizes healthy living through diet and physical and spiritual fitness.

Orthodox Christian (Orthodox Catholic or Eastern Orthodox)

The perfect person does good through love.

–St. Clement of Alexandria

Although the Greek Orthodox Church is the Orthodox denomination with the largest membership in the United States, there are several others, including Romanian, Serbian, Russian, and Ukrainian. Orthodox services may be held in the language of the country or of the congregation. Hierarchal and self-governing, the churches are called "Eastern" because they originated in countries that shared the Christian heritage of the eastern part of the Byzantine/Roman Empire. The beliefs of the Orthodox Christian Church are similar to those of other Christian traditions.

The Orthodox cross, known as the tri-bar cross, differs from that of Western Christianity. The top bar often bears the letters INBI or INRI, acronyms of the Greek and Latin translations of "Jesus of Nazareth, King of the Jews". Icons, a major focus of devotion, can be found in Orthodox cathedrals, churches, and homes.

SERVICES AND CEREMONIES

The traditional posture for prayer and worship is to stand. In old Orthodox churches, there are no pews, only benches or chairs along the sidewalls for the elderly and infirm. Guests may also use these but should stand during the entrances of the priests, gospel readings, the blessings of priests, Holy Communion, and the Dismissal.

❖ **Basic Service:** The Sunday service, the Divine Liturgy, is the weekly celebration of the Eucharist. When entering the church, the worshippers light one or two candles and place them in a candle stand. They then move around to the various icons, making the sign of the cross at each and touching the floor.

The service, consisting of nine sections and various litanies, generally lasts for at least two hours. As the priest enters and speaks, all worshippers stand and bow their heads. Except for a sermon, most of the service is sung or intoned without instrumental accompaniment. When references are made to the Father, Son, saints, etc., worshippers may cross themselves and touch the floor with their right hand.

Most worshipers remain standing for the entire service, but guests are welcome to sit, if necessary. Congregants may leave the church to go outside during the service. Throughout the service, the priest will pass by carrying a golden censer, which emits clouds of incense. As he blesses icons and worshippers, slightly bow your head. You may wish to participate in the offertory. The notes/papers that people hand to the deacons contain the names of those they wish to be commemorated in the Liturgy. Many churches have pamphlets or books in the pews that help guests follow the service.

The end of the service, the Dismissal, is marked by the priest's holding up the cross for worshipers to kiss before receiving a second piece of blessed bread. Because other rituals and occasions might be observed following the Divine Liturgy service, it can sometimes be difficult to know when it has actually ended.

A short reception of light food in a room of the church usually follows the service.

❖ **Marriage Ceremonies:** Most Orthodox marriage ceremonies are steeped in Byzantine rituals and are rich with scriptural symbolism. The ceremony, usually held on a Saturday or Sunday, consists of two main parts and may last as long as two hours. The priest presides, and the couple has attendants to assist them and carry the matrimonial crowns.

The first part, the betrothal (the Exchange of Rings), may be celebrated out of view in the narthex (vestibule) of the church. In addition to blessing the couple and their marriage, the priest conducts a ring ceremony. He exchanges the rings three times signifying that their lives are forever entwined and places them on their right-hand ring fingers. (In the Bible, the right hand is the "good" and preferred hand.) After offering a prayer and chanting the Marriage Psalm, the priest leads the procession into the main part of the church for the marriage ceremony.

The second part, the crowning (the Order of Marriage or Sacrament of Holy Matrimony), begins with the lighting of candles, litanies, and prayers. The attendants hand the wedding crowns to the priest, who places them on their respective heads as he repeats a blessing. The crowns, which may be actual golden crowns (Russian) or wreaths of flowers (Greek), are rich in symbolism. Traditional music can be used for the processional and recessional, but ancient hymns, rituals, and chants are used throughout the service.

The crowning service continues with readings from the Epistle and the Gospel, the Common Cup (sharing of wine by couple), and the Dance of Isaiah. Near the end of the service, the crowns are removed, and the priest prays that God will receive these crowns. In remembrance of the Trinity, things are done in threes throughout the service. Following the benedictions, the couple turns around to face the congregation for the Greeting of the Couple. The assembly comes up to congratulate them.

The celebratory reception that follows may be held in the same building as the ceremony, the bride's parents' home, a catering hall, or other venue. You may bring gifts to the wedding or the reception or send them to the home of the newlyweds.

❖ **Mourning and Funerals:** In the Orthodox Church, death is a transformation, often referred to as dormition, which means "falling asleep." There is great respect for the body; and the washing and the dressing of the deceased are significant. Mourning and funeral rituals are an important tradition, even though Orthodox churches have different funeral rites, each mirroring its own beliefs and culture. Prior to the funeral, friends may visit the family to offer condolences.

The Orthodox funeral consists of three different services: the Vigil Service, the Trisagion (which is usually performed at the church or funeral home the evening before the day of the funeral), and the actual funeral (which usually takes place within two or three days after death: three days for Russian Orthodox). The funeral itself is usually held at either the church or a funeral home with an open casket. Viewing the body, however, is optional. Christians may kiss the cross or icon resting on the casket. The program may include celebration of the Divine Liturgy. Non-Orthodox guests should not participate in Holy Communion. At the interment, the Trisagion service is repeated, and the officiant prays and places soil on top of the casket in the shape of a cross. Before leaving the site, each person places a single flower on the casket. Lamentation both in the house and at the cemetery is a significant part of some Orthodox funerals.

There is usually a post-funeral gathering in another location that guests may attend. Traditional foods are served and shared. Cards and letters of condolence or flowers may be sent as well as requested donations, which often go to the deceased's church. The memorial service is repeated throughout the first year and usually at the end of the forty-day mourning period as well as on annual anniversaries.

DRESS

Dress modestly. Some churches (especially Russian Orthodox) require head coverings, so women should bring shawls or scarves. Women should not wear trousers. Always wear black to an Orthodox Christian funeral, as this is the color of mourning.

PARTICIPATION

Non-Orthodox guests may participate in reading prayers and singing but not Holy Communion. Trays will be passed for an offertory.

- ❖ Enter or leave a ceremony during Scripture readings and blessings.

- ❖ Take Holy Communion unless you are an Orthodox Christian.

LEXICON

CENSER: Incense holder.

ICONS: Religious works of art, usually of holy beings, objects, or stories.

ICONOSTASIS: A long, ornate, icon-covered screen that extends the length of the church and contains three doors, each giving access to special areas.

KLOBUK: Clerical headgear covered with a draped veil worn by Orthodox clergy; various colors and decoration indicate rank and honor within the clerical hierarchy.

LITANIES: Responsorial, repetitive prayers.

LITURGY: Rite or body of rites prescribed for public worship.

PASCHA: Easter.

PRESBYTER: Priest.

PROSPHORA: Individual offerings of loaves of bread.

Other Denominational Experiences

Information about certain customs, rituals, and language, unique to certain faiths, may help guests to become more comfortable in a new environment.

Baha'i Faith

❖ Although their regular worship service combined with a business meeting is usually restricted to members of the faith, guests may be invited to attend. Their service, called the Nineteen-Day Feast (meaning a spiritual feast) is held on the first day of each of the nineteen months of the Baha'i calendar. They also hold other smaller meetings in homes and community centers.

❖ Baha'is celebrate the New Year on March 21, the spring equinox. Most do not attend school or work on this holiday.

❖ Funeral rituals ban embalming the body unless required by state law. The deceased must be buried within one hour's travel time from the place of death. Non-Baha'i individuals cannot contribute to a Baha'i fund.

❖ Guests, invited by a Native person to a particular ceremony, should first prepare by learning about the ceremony and the spirituality and concepts that underlie its rituals. Invitations could be for the Sun Dance Ceremony, Potlatch Ceremony, Sweat Lodge Ceremony, Stomp Ceremony, Blessingway Ceremony, or a seasonal ceremony.

❖ As many of these are held outside—some at sacred sites— dress for the weather and climate. Be prepared to stand and sit still for long periods. Show your respect by being quiet, paying attention, and not asking questions about the meaning of things or the symbolism invoked. Native people believe that the Creator gave all human beings knowledge of the sacred.

Pentecostal Church of God

❖ Guests should expect very exuberant services, which may include prayers, music, readings, and "praying in tongues." The service may include foot washing, with persons washing the feet of others of the same gender.

Quaker: Religious Society of Friends

❖ The Friends have two types of meetings (services): unprogrammed or silent meetings, where persons will sit in silence unless they receive divine guidance to speak or sing, and programmed meetings, which are planned and led by a pastor. Either type of meeting can be a part of a marriage ceremony or a funeral. Do not leave during a meeting and do not speak during an unprogrammed meeting unless you feel deeply moved and have something of value to share with others.

❖ Many Quakers do not celebrate holidays, such as Christmas and Easter, because they believe that every day is a holy day.

Seventh-Day Adventist

❖ The basic religious service is held on Saturday mornings (the Sabbath). They also avoid labor and many secular activities for the day. Sabbath School is a study service, which precedes the regular worship service. Adventists do not recognize any religious holidays except the Sabbath.

❖ There is always a foot-washing ritual in which men and women separate to wash one another's feet in different rooms/areas. Guests may participate or remain in the sanctuary.

❖ For a funeral, it is appropriate to send cards or letters of condolence and to send flowers to the deceased's home or to the funeral; however, it is not appropriate to make a donation in the person's name or honor.

Sikh

❖ A Sikh community can be identified by the orange- or saffron-colored flag that displays the *Khanda* emblem of interlocking swords. Sunday is the main day of worship, and men and women may be seated separately. A *gurdwara* (gateway to the guru) is anywhere a service takes place—someone's home, special building or room, or temple. An act of devotion, preparing and cooking food for the congregation, is part of the service.

❖ Guests should wear modest clothing, comfortable enough to sit on the floor cross-legged for a couple of hours. Remove shoes before entering the presence of the Holy Scriptures; you may leave on socks, if necessary. Washing your hands and feet is optional. The top of the head must be kept covered. Women use a scarf or stole; men without hats will be offered a *patka* cloth to tie over their heads.

❖ On first entering, all should make a small bow to the Guru Granth Sahib (Holy Book). Visitors may place an offering of money in the container provided when they arrive or leave. Sit on the floor, facing the front, making sure that your feet face away from the Guru Granth Sahib. Guests will be offered *prasad* (sweet flour and oil–based food), which will be placed into their cupped hands. It is a good idea to bring hand wipes with you. Always eat the food with the right hand. Refrain from any unnecessary conversation.

❖ When leaving the *gurdwara*, do not abruptly turn your back on the holy book, but bow slightly and then take a few steps backward before turning to leave.

PART SEVEN
REGISTERING SOCIALLY

Concerts: Opera, Symphony, Ballet, and Jazz

Music is the one incorporeal entrance into the higher world of knowledge which comprehends mankind about which mankind cannot comprehend.

–Ludwig van Beethoven

WHAT YOU NEED TO KNOW

The considerate concertgoer will not arrive late or get up between acts; unwrap or crunch food or candy; open anything with Velcro; turn on anything that beeps; take photographs or record; talk or whisper during the performance; obstruct another's view with a hat, large hair, or nuzzling with one's date; bounce one's head up and down to the music; applaud while the conductor is facing the orchestra; or leave before the performers' curtain calls.

OPERA

❖ If invited to the opera, you need not wear formal or semi-formal attire unless you are attending an opening night or other special gala. Many attend in business attire—dark suits for men and dresses or suits for women. Despite the increasing trend toward informality, ripped jeans and shredded T-shirts are definitely not appropriate and demonstrate little respect for performers, the institution, and fellow concertgoers.

❖ If seated in someone's box, you will usually hang your coat once you enter the box rather than at the general coat check. The host or owner of the box usually occupies the least desirable seat, giving the seat with the best view to the eldest or most distinguished guest.

❖ Prior to the event, learn something about the story, composer, music, and history of the opera as well as about the featured stars and the conductor.

❖ Arrive early, or you will have to wait until after the overture—or maybe the first act—before being seated. It's best to use bathroom before the show starts, as lines between acts can become very long.

❖ Clap when the conductor comes out to start the overture, at the end of an act or the end of the opera while the singers are taking bows, and when everyone else around you is clapping, such as after an aria.

❖ To help the audience understand what is going on, many opera houses have "supertitles," translations that are projected on a screen above the stage. Some are in English. A few houses, such as the Metropolitan Opera, have individual screens on the backs of the seats in front of you, enabling you to turn them on and off. Most programs will include a brief synopsis of the action by act that you can also refer to.

SYMPHONY

❖ An orchestra is divided into four families of instruments: strings, woodwinds, brass, and percussion. Each family has its own section in an orchestra, and each has its own responsibility in creating the sound of the orchestra. Each section has a principal who is responsible for leading the group as well as for playing orchestral solos.

❖ Orchestral protocol: Members enter and tune instruments prior to show; when instruments become quiet, the conductor enters usually to applause; the conductor nods to audience, who become quiet, and then turns to face the orchestra and raises the baton to signal the start of the overture/musical performance.

BALLET

❖ Ballet is a classical dance form that creates expression through formalized steps and gestures set in graceful, flowing patterns. As a theatrical entertainment, it is usually combined with orchestral music, costumes, and scenery to tell a story.

❖ The essential element is the visual spectacle. Because ballet performers tell stories with body movements, not words, learn about the ballet you are planning to see and take the time to read plot summaries and critical reviews as well as information about the principal dancers, or "stars," of the particular performance.

❖ Don't be surprised at the amount of sound dancers generate in real life; the noises made by tapping pointe shoes, jumping, and even heavy breathing can be disconcerting at first.

❖ In balletiquette, the audience applauds when the conduc
tor appears, when a principal appears onstage for the first
time, when a dancer bows, and at the end of an impressive
series of movements or sequence of steps. After particularly
moving performances, "bravo," "brava," and "bravi" are also
shouted during the applause.

JAZZ

❖ Whether the concert has open seating or more formal
assigned seating, audience members are expected to clap
when the band and players first come out, after each number, and when the set concludes. Clapping at the end of
each solo is also encouraged.

❖ Improvisation (improv) is an important aspect of jazz and
one that distinguishes it from other forms of music. It is
music created spontaneously and in the moment—without
a written score and not played from memory.

WHAT YOU MAY WANT TO KNOW

OPERA

❖ Stage directions and positions: Stage right and left refer
to the division of the stage from the performer's point of
view, not the audience's point of view. Upstage and downstage refer to the position on stage farthest or nearest the
audience with downstage meaning that the performer is
moving toward the audience and upstage, away from the
audience.

❖ Bravo guide:

- o BRAVO to a single male performer's exceptional performance.

- o BRAVA to a single female's exceptional performance.

- o BRAVI (brah-VEE) to a group of all male performers or a mix of male and female performers' exceptional performances.

- o BRAVE (brah-VAY) to a group of all female performers' exceptional performances. Occasionally, the superlative form.

- o BRAVISSIMO is used for an unusually exceptional performance.

SYMPHONY

- ❖ The audience may talk freely until the end of the applause that greets the entrance of the conductor—or the entrance of the concertmaster if the orchestra tunes onstage.

- ❖ It is common for audience to quietly reflect in respectful silence before applauding after performances of sacred works, including requiems, Masses, etc. And often, after a quiet finale such as Tchaikovsky's *Pathétique* Symphony, applause does not begin immediately.

BALLET

- ❖ A great way to familiarize yourself with a ballet is to listen to the music prior to the performance. Music of most classical ballets can be found online or on CDs.

- ❖ Reading the program will provide you with interesting facts about the ballet, the ballet company, and its past performances.

- ❖ There are three major styles of ballet: classical, the most formal, adhering to traditional ballet technique; neoclassical, traditional but less rigid than classical; and contemporary, influenced by both classical ballet and modern dance.

- ❖ The most famous ballets: *Swan Lake, Cinderella, Sleeping Beauty, The Nutcracker, Romeo and Juliet, Giselle, Don Quixote, A Midsummer's Night Dream, La Bayadère* (The Temple Dancer), and *Le Sacre du Printemps* (The Rite of Spring).

JAZZ

- ❖ In general, when several soloists play in rapid succession, there is a progression with the lead or featured player playing last. Thus, there is usually a progression also in the volume and duration of clapping after each solo.

- ❖ Respect the musicians and the audience. If you are late to the concert, move quickly and quietly to a position that does not distract the musicians or audience members—even if it means standing until the number is finished.

WHAT YOU MAY FIND HELPFUL TO KNOW

BALLET

- ❖ If this is your first ballet and you have a choice, you might prefer a mixed program to one full-length ballet. The program usually consists of three short distinct pieces, enabling you to discover more about your personal taste.

❖ Not all productions are equal. There are various versions with many different sets and costumes—also some are full-length while others are shortened.

❖ Traditionally, when dancers exit through the stage door after the performance, they will give autographs—and maybe some photo opportunities.

WHAT NOT TO DO

OPERA

❖ Do not interrupt with questions, act bored, applaud at the wrong time, doze off, or forget to thank your host.

❖ Do not whistle (unless in the United Kingdom). In some cultures, such as Italy, it is equivalent to booing.

SYMPHONY

❖ Do not applaud between movements of a symphony no matter how much you enjoyed the music—it is considered a faux pas. The conductor lowers his hands when the performance has ended.

BALLET

❖ Do not bring young children who cannot sit quietly in their own seats and observe a two-hour performance without talking. Most ballet companies recommend that children be at least five years old to attend performances of

The Nutcracker and eight years old to attend regular performances.

JAZZ

❖ Although you are encouraged to applaud after a solo or improvisation, do not interrupt an improvisation by whispering, moving around, etc., as the musician is spontaneously expressing his own emotions.

❖ Do not yell after a solo or song. Occasionally—in an informal venue—you may hear "yeah"; however, these are usually shouted by their friends or regulars.

LEXICON
OPERA

APRON: Front part of the stage between the curtain and the orchestra pit.

ARIA: Solo voice with instrumental accompaniment within an opera or operetta.

BARITONE: Medium male voice between the lower bass and the higher tenor.

BASS: Lowest male voice.

BEL CANTO: Type of lyrical singing associated with nineteenth-century opera. Literally translates to "beautiful singing."

CADENZA: Series of difficult, fast high notes that allow the singer to demonstrate vocal ability; usually at the end of an aria.

COLORATURA SOPRANO: Virtuoso, high-pitched, fast singing with trills and embellishments.

CONTRALTO: Lowest female voice part, between soprano and tenor.

DIVA: "Goddess" or opera star.

FALSETTO: The high-pitched part of a man's voice, in which he sounds like a woman.

FINALE: Last song of an act, usually involving many singers.

GRAND OPERA: Opera that is entirely sung, with no spoken dialogue.

LIBRETTO: Text of an opera.

MAESTRO: Meaning "master," a courtesy title given to conductors, composers, and directors.

MEZZO SOPRANO: Female voice between the higher soprano and the lower contralto.

OPERA BUFFA: Comic opera.

OPERA COMIQUE: Opera in which there is some spoken dialogue.

OPERETTA: Light opera that includes dialogue.

OVERTURE: Introduction to an opera or other large musical work.

PRIMA DONNA: Female opera star ("first lady").

RANGE: The division of human voice into six basic types—soprano, mezzo soprano, contralto, tenor, baritone, and bass.

RECITATIVE: Vocal style used for dialogue/narrative in opera.

SOPRANO: Highest female voice.

SUPERNUMERARY: A performer who does not sing.

TENOR: Highest male voice.

VERISMO: Form of Italian opera about everyday life set in composer's own time.

VIBRATO: Wavering quality of a sustained note.

SYMPHONY LEXICON

ADAGIO: Slow, restful tempo.

ALLEGRO: Lively and fast tempo.

BAROQUE: Emotional, flowery music.

CADENZA: A succession of chords that brings an end to a musical phrase.

CAPRICCIO: A short, quick, spirited improvisational piece of music.

CHAMBER ORCHESTRA/MUSIC: Small ensemble or the music written for it.

CLASSICAL: The music period from roughly the mid-1700s to the early 1800s.

CONCERT MASTER: The first violinist in an orchestra who is the leader of not only the string section but of the entire orchestra, subordinate only to the conductor. Concertgoers may observe the concertmaster leading the tuning of the orchestra prior to a concert.

CONCERTO: A composition for soloist and orchestra.

CRESCENDO: Getting progressively louder.

DIMINUENDO: Getting progressively softer.

DUET: A musical composition for two performers: two voices, same instruments or different instruments.

ENCORE: Request to play again/more.

ETUDE: A study or exercise for improving technique.

FINALE: Last section or movement of symphony, sonata, or ending of opera.

FORTE: Symbol meaning to play loudly.

INTERMEZZO: Short interlude connecting the main parts of a composition.

MAJOR: One of the two modes of the musical tonal system. Music written in major keys is positive and affirming.

MINOR: One of the two modes of the musical tonal system. Music written in minor keys is likely to be dark or melancholy.

MOVEMENT: A section of a larger composition.

NOCTURNE: Dreamy, romantic musical composition.

OPUS: A single work or composition with number to show order in which piece was written or published.

ORCHESTRATION: Study of writing music; also the act of arranging and using instruments to achieve maximum effect.

PHILHARMONIC: Music loving or appreciative of music in reference to a symphony orchestra; can be used interchangeably with "symphony" to name an orchestra.

PIZZICATO: Picking string instruments instead of bowing them.

REPRISE: To repeat a previous part of a composition.

SCALE: Successive notes of a key or mode either ascending or descending.

SONATA: Music with four movements, each of which differs in tempo, rhythm, and melody but held together by subject and style.

STRING QUARTET: Instrumental group consisting of two violins, a viola, and a cello.

TEMPO: The speed of a musical passage.

TUNING: Raising or lowering the pitch of an instrument to produce the correct tone of a note.

VIRTUOSO (noun or adjective): Playing with exceptional ability, artistry, and/or technique.

BALLET LEXICON

ARABESQUE: A position in which you balance on one straight or bent leg, stretching the other out behind you.

BALLERINA: Female professional ballet dancer.

BALLET CORPS: Ensemble cast of dancers.

BARRE: Horizontal wooden handrail used to exercise and practice.

CHOREOGRAPHY: The art of creating and arranging dances as well as planning the movements and steps of the dancers.

GLISSADE: Gliding or sliding traveling steps.

JETE: A ballet leap in which the weight of the dancer is transferred from one foot to the other.

PAS DE DEUX: A ballet duet.

PIROUETTE: A full turn of the body on the point of the toe or the ball of the foot.

PLIE: Exercise by moving up and down with a bend of the knees while keeping back straight;

POINTE: A position of the foot in which your heel is held up, your big toe is stretched down, your leg is turned out, and your foot is on line with your leg.

PRIMA BALLERINA: Title or rank given to the most notable ballerinas.

PRINCIPAL: Dancer at the highest level within a professional dance company; can be a man or woman.

ROUTINE: Dance term meaning sequence of steps.

AXE: Slang term for electric guitar, sometimes used for other instruments as well.

BEAT: The pronounced rhythm of music.

BREAK: Transitional passage in which a soloist plays without accompaniment.

COMBO: Abbreviation for "combination" (of instruments).

COOL JAZZ: Modern, more relaxed jazz style (circa 1950) characterized by moderate volume, quiet rhythm sections, low vibrato, and often incorporating elements of classical music.

FALSE FINGERING: Technique of finger placement that produces tones/sounds not possible using orthodox techniques.

GIG: Slang for a paying musical engagement—usually for a short term, often just one evening.

HORN: Term used to refer generally to any brass instrument.

JAM (SESSIONS): Improvised solos over well-known standard compositions, with the outcome depending solely on the shared knowledge and ability of the players.

LIP: Strength and ability of brass players to execute music, especially high notes.

ORGAN TRIO: Three musicians featuring a Hammond organ player with two other musicians.

RIFF: Supporting solo of repeated short melodic phrases that function rhythmically, usually rapid and energetic.

SESSION MUSICIAN: Experienced, skilled musician who is hired for recording sessions.

SIDEMAN: Musician who accompanies the lead singer or instrumentalist.

SIT-IN: Musician invited to perform on stage with performing group for one or more songs: sometimes improvisational.

SMOOTH JAZZ: Fusion in which elements or rhythm and blues, funk, and pop music are distilled (mainly by the constraints of radio) to become recognizable melodies.

SYNCOPATION: Playing off the main rhythm and interrupting the regular beat.

TRAIN WRECK: Slang term for when a major event (usually error by a performer) negatively affects a performance.

VAMP: A repeated chord progression and/or rhythm leading into or out of a tune or composition.

Art Auctions

You like it, that's all, whether it's a landscape or abstract.
You like it. It hits you. You don't have to read it. The work
of art—sculpture or painting—forces your eye.

– Clement Greenberg, art critic

That more people are becoming knowledgeable about and interested in art does not mean that they are comfortable at an art auction. A rarified part of the art world, auction houses have their own practices, jargon, and etiquette. For the novice, ignorance about accepted audience etiquette results in social blundering and discomfort. Although much of the information here is specific to the sale of various types of art work (i.e., paintings, drawings, jewelry, coins, sculpture, and antiques) in auction houses, much of the terminology and knowledge is applicable to other, less formal, types of auctions—even live online auctions.

Many nonprofits raise money by holding art auctions. These auctions range from those conducted by trained, well-informed auctioneers to auctions arranged and conducted by employees/volunteers of the charity. These events can be an excellent way for nonprofits to raise money, for artist donors to receive free publicity, and for bidders to get quality art at reasonable prices. Some artists, however, are boycotting these auctions, believing that they have depressed the value of art across the board, keeping artists in a subordinate position.

❖ Do your homework about the period, the artist, the work, and its condition.

❖ Read the catalog carefully—you can also use an artist's previous sales and online auction databases.

❖ If possible, attend the preview to thoroughly inspect all items of interest.

❖ Register yourself and obtain your personal paddle number prior to the auction. You will be required to provide your photo ID and basic banking information so they know who you are.

❖ Become knowledgeable about the rules and regulations governing the auction.

❖ Your numbered paddle is your only official identification, deploy it wisely and judiciously to draw the attention of the auctioneer to you when you wish to bid or purchase.

❖ Although it is wise to try to get a good seat, realize you may not be able to sit wherever you wish, as auction houses frequently use seating charts, fine-tuning them until the last minute.

WHAT YOU MAY WANT TO KNOW

❖ You will observe continual low-volume discussion between buyers and their advisors, many standing around the edges of the room so that they can leave to converse outside.

❖ A bid spotter can be a good ally. Remote bidding (by phone) can be convenient and discreet, but because you are using an intermediary, you cannot move as quickly and you cannot "read" the room.

❖ Absentee bids are common. Bidders fill out a form listing their highest bids, and the auction house then competitively bids on their behalf.

❖ The true connoisseur will know and/or meet with the dealers, find out the unpublished reserve price, and know who might be bidding for a particular piece.

WHAT YOU MAY FIND HELPFUL TO KNOW

❖ Some persons bid by phone—through the phone bank—but are also there in person.

❖ Learn when to applaud, whether it's for a record sale or about the significance of the object being auctioned.

❖ Congratulate the successful winner.

❖ The less experienced, unsophisticated bidders can be recognized because they frequently enter the bidding early and then bid almost automatically.

WHAT NOT TO DO

❖ Use a cell phone during the bidding.

❖ Ask a fellow bidder about a certain item and then bid against the person for the item.

❖ Bid on something you do not want to buy.

LEXICON

APPRAISAL: The evaluation of an object's monetary worth.

AUCTIONEER: Individual who conducts the sales at auctions. Standing in front of potential buyers, the auctioneer describes the items and then takes bids, utilizing a specific fast-paced lingo.

AUCTION HOUSE: Business that operates contractually on behalf of sellers of goods.

BID: Offer to purchase the item being sold.

BIDDING INCREMENTS: The system of predetermined bid increases that the bidding follows during an auction. Beware, however, this process has its vagaries.

BID SPOTTER: House employees who provide prospective bidders with information about the lots. They stand to the side of the rostrum, scanning their section for bids and potential bids, relaying bid information to the auctioneer and identifying the top bidder. Also called the ring man or ground man.

BOUGHT IN: When a lot/item does not sell, it remains the property of the owner—it is "bought in."

BUYER'S PREMIUM: A surcharge of a stated percentage added to the highest bid. This fee is added to the "hammer price."

CATALOGUE: List and description of artworks to be sold; it is written and usually available well before the auction date.

EXECUTE A BID: The process of bidding.

GUARANTEED MINIMUM: Guaranteed selling price offered to sellers; it also gives reassurance to potential bidders that the item is in demand.

KNOCKED DOWN: When the lot is sold, the auctioneer's hammer comes down. The term means that it has been sold.

LOT: A group of objects offered for sale as one entity. Each offering by the auctioneer is one lot.

ORDER BID: A written or verbal bid made by the auction house on the bidder's behalf.

PADDLE: A numbered flat instrument used to signal bids at auctions.

PRE-SALE ESTIMATE: The price range within which the auction house estimates the object/lot will most likely sell.

PREVIEW: A designated period for prospective bidders to view and inspect the property to be offered for sale.

RESERVE PRICE: The lowest price a seller will accept, usually agreed on confidentially between the seller and the auction house.

ROCK: A bidder who won't quit.

Afternoon Tea

Under certain circumstances, there are few hours more
agreeable than the hour dedicated to the ceremony known
as afternoon tea.

—Henry James, The Portrait of a Lady

Americans frequently refer to afternoon tea as high tea; however, high tea or meat tea in Britain tends to be a later, heavier meal, such as dinner. Afternoon tea, usually served at four or five o'clock, is also called low tea because it was served in a room with low tables and sofas, settees, or stuffed chairs.

WHAT YOU NEED TO KNOW

❖ There are three types of afternoon tea: cream tea, served with scones accompanied by jam and clotted or Devonshire cream; light tea, served with scones and sweets; and full tea, served with savories, scones, sweets, and dessert.

❖ Depending on how tea is being prepared and served, the host may need a tea pot, strainer, infuser, milk pitcher, tea scoop, tea caddy, very hot water in a kettle or urn, sugar tongs or sugar spoon, lemon, small forks, and twelve-inch cloth napkins (traditionally white).

❖ Always serve milk, not cream, with tea, as it is too heavy. It is best to pour the milk in after the tea has been poured, not before.

❖ Always remove the teabag from the cup and place it on the saucer.

❖ Hold handled teacups by placing fingers to the front and back of the handle. Do not stick your "pinkie" up in the air—rather, use it for better balance.

❖ If serving lemon, also provide a small fork for guests unless a server can place the lemon into the cup after pouring the tea.

❖ The only time a saucer is raised together with the teacup is when one is at a standing reception.

WHAT YOU MAY WANT TO KNOW

❖ The spout of the teapot or kettle should face the host/pourer when on the table.

❖ Most English tearooms serve afternoon tea from three to five o'clock and offer courses of savories, scones, and pastries/sweets. In addition to a wide variety of traditional teas, many now also serve herbal teas and infusions.

❖ Popular teas include black tea, made from fermented leaves of tea plants; Oolong tea, made from semi-fermented leaves of tea plants; green tea, which has not yet been oxidized and thus has more health benefits; white tea, which is made from early buds of tea plants; tisanes, which are herbal teas; and compressed tea, which is tea pressed into brick-like shapes.

❖ Both the Palm Court at the Plaza in New York City and the Palm Court at the Park Lane in London are famous for their traditional, elaborate afternoon teas.

❖ For festive occasions, champagne and sherry can also be served at the end of afternoon tea.

WHAT YOU MAY FIND HELPFUL TO KNOW

❖ The term "take tea" was used by the lower classes during the Victorian era and thus was considered a vulgar expression. "Drink tea" is still more acceptable.

❖ To eat a scone, break off a bite-size piece and then spread jam and cream. Do not use a fork.

❖ When serving lemon with tea, slices are preferable to wedges. The lemon slice can float in the teacup; the squeezed wedge is placed on tea saucer or the service plate provided.

❖ Although modern food choices and placement vary greatly, the three-tiered curate stand traditionally holds scones on the top tier, savories and tea sandwiches on the middle tier, and sweets on the bottom tier. Sometimes the top tier is covered to keep scones warm.

❖ In the mid-eighteenth century, after tea was introduced to Britain, dinner for the upper and middle classes shifted from noontime to a "fashionably late," heavier, longer meal in the evening. To counteract the effects of the skimpier midday meal, the (hungry) Duchess of Bedford had her servant bring her tea and snacks each afternoon. Soon she began inviting her friends for this additional meal, and the practice became extremely popular with Britain's more social hostesses.

❖ Tea dances are still a popular pastime in Britain. Usually held on Sunday afternoons from two to five o'clock, live bands play ballroom classics while beautifully dressed couples enjoy afternoon tea with their waltzes.

❖ The annual Newport Vintage Dance Week in Rhode Island includes tea dances—some with costumes and classes.

❖ The Japanese tea ceremony, called the Way of Tea, is the art of ceremonial tea drinking. Steeped in Zen tradition and highly stylized, the ceremony is a hospitable cultural activity relating to the pursuit of truth and beauty.

WHAT NOT TO DO

❖ Serve cream with tea.

❖ Add both lemon and milk, as the citric acid in the lemon will curdle the proteins in the milk.

❖ Stir your tea with large circular motions.

❖ Slurp or use tea to wash down your food.

❖ Loop your fingers through the handles of the cup and/or hold it with the palm of your hand.

❖ Leave your teaspoon in your teacup.

- ❖ Hold your teacup up in the air or wave it around.

- ❖ Use the string of a tea bag to squeeze it out.

- ❖ Slice a scone, although some may be served pre-sliced with jam and cream.

LEXICON

ASSAM: The world's largest black tea producing region, located in northeastern India. The tea is deep dark red in color.

CAMBRIC TEA: A weakly infused tea with large amounts of milk and sugar.

CURATE STAND/BUTLER'S STAND: Consists of three different porcelain dishes, each a different size with the smallest on the top.

DARJEELING: A tea-growing region of India, located just south of Nepal, that produces the "champagne of teas."

INFUSION: Tea's liquid extract, prepared by steeping.

SAVORIES: Nonsweet foods traditionally served with afternoon tea.

SCONE: Small, round, or triangular biscuit-like quick bread or pastry.

STEEP: To soak in liquid; to infuse.

WINE TASTING

Quickly, bring me a beaker of wine that I may wet my mind and say something clever.

–Aristophanes

I f wine tasting is a new experience for you—whether at a winery, restaurant, wine shop, a private wine cellar, or a special wine tasting venue with individual light boxes and sinks—remember that wine tasting is a shared communal activity where all opinions should be taken into account. Always respect the wine: drink it slowly and give it time to reveal its true nature.

Wine tastings are structured in many different ways: by grape varietal, wine region, producer (vertical), or vintage (horizontal). A tasting may be blind, thematic, paired with selected foods, or organized as a wine scoring (rating) experience.

Tasting skills are easy to learn

1. Observe: Enjoy the color and clarity of the wine.
2. Swirl and sniff: Place glass on flat surface and grasp stem swirling to stoke (aerate) and liberate the aromas.
3. Sip: Lifting wine glass, sip and move wine around your palate, sucking in air to "liberate" its perfume.

4. Spit or swallow: If you are tasting/learning about multiple wines, you can spit out a sample after rolling it around on your tongue a few times. For discreet spitting, request an individual spittoon or cup and leave the larger collective buckets for dumping excess from your glass or from your individual spittoon.

5. Enjoy the finish: Pay attention to the aftertaste and the lingering flavor.

6. Ask questions: Indicate an interest in the wines, the process, and the history.

If you wish to sample a wine that you have previously tasted, ask your server if you may "please revisit" that particular wine. Reserve wines are a winery's more exclusive, limited production offerings.

WHAT NOT TO DO

❖ Go wine tasting on an empty stomach.

❖ Hold your wine glass by the bowl as greasy fingerprints are repugnant and can disturb the wine's temperature.

❖ Chug or gulp wine.

❖ "Hog" the wine—share.

❖ Wear perfume or heavily scented cologne, aftershave, or lotions.

❖ Brush your teeth with flavored toothpaste immediately before tasting.

❖ Miss the spittoon or spit bucket.

Bows and Curtsies

Alice: "But I was just thinking." Queen of Hearts:
"Curtsy while you're thinking. It saves time."
                              –Lewis Carroll, *Alice in Wonderland*

BOWS

WHAT YOU NEED TO KNOW

❖ In some cultures, the bow is the equivalent of a handshake.

❖ Deeply ingrained in Asian cultures and characteristic of nobility/aristocracy in European countries, bowing is the act of lowering the head and, usually, the torso as a social gesture of courtesy to a person or symbol.

❖ In Asian cultures, always respond to a bow with a bow.

❖ Because the depth of a bow indicates the relationship between the individuals, always observe the depth of a bow and respond appropriately: to an equal, with the same depth; to a superior, with a deeper bow; and to one of lower status, a shallower bow.

- The longer and deeper the bow, the greater the difference in status and/or the stronger the emotion being expressed.

- A traditional Indian and Thai greeting is a slight bow with palms of hands pressed together, as though praying.

- Lower your eyes when bowing.

- It is not necessary in the United States to bow or curtsy when meeting visiting royalty; however, they may be performed as an act of courtesy if accomplished with grace.

- Depending on the country and the culture, in international business greetings, the bow is often combined with a handshake.

WHAT YOU MAY WANT TO KNOW

- In Asian cultures, business cards are presented after the bow and are handed to the recipient so that the card is oriented facing the recipient and with the most appropriate language facing up.

- There are many types of bows: of greeting and departing, as an integral part of martial arts practices, performed during tea ceremonies, of reverence, of varying degrees of apology, or thanks, and also religious bows (including in Hindu, Shinto, Buddhism, Islam, Christian, and Judaism).

- Bows are sometimes used instead of speaking, such as in replacing a casual "hello" or "hi" when passing. Throughout Asia, bows are also used to express gratitude, remorse, sincerity, deference, or humility—either in private or in public. You may have observed news conferences in which government officials or industry leaders bow deeply to show remorse or shame. (These bows usually take place behind a table with the apologetic individual lowering his body from the waist until his face is parallel with the tabletop.)

❖ Genuflection, the act of bending a knee to the ground and immediately rising, is used in various religious rites and liturgies. It is also used in Western cultures for proposing marriage.

WHAT YOU MIGHT FIND HELPFUL TO KNOW

❖ In Japan, the degree of the bow is as important as the action itself. There are three degrees: the 45 degree bow with palms in front of knees, the 35 degree bow with legs straight and hands at sides, and the informal bow, a quick, slight bowing of head and shoulders sometimes used before shaking hands with a Westerner.

❖ In a tea ceremony, bows are exchanged repeatedly—at the beginning, end, and throughout. Students learn three main types of bow, when to perform each, and with whom each is appropriately performed.

❖ In Japan if two friends or relatives have been separated for some time, when they finally meet, they bow to each other numerous times, not exchanging a word.

WHAT NOT TO DO

❖ Bump heads when bowing.

❖ If female, do not make eye contact with a male while bowing.

CURTSIES

WHAT YOU NEED TO KNOW

❖ A curtsy is a gesture of respect that is made by a woman. It is used when being introduced to someone of high rank or social status and during very formal occasions. The more important the person, the more elaborate the curtsy.

❖ An informal or simple curtsy consists of bending the knees while bowing the head.

❖ How to curtsy correctly:

❖ 1) Lower your head; 2) Place your hands on the sides of your skirt, and hold it out sideways (if your skirt is too narrow, then hold your hands out to your sides with palms facing upward); 3) Extend your right foot a few inches behind the left so that your right knee is slightly bent; 4) For a more formal curtsy, bend your knees outward, rather than forward, bowing your head and shoulders and lowering yourself evenly; and 5) Bring yourself gracefully to your original standing position.

❖ Most curtsies last only one or two seconds.

❖ Maintain eye contact during the curtsy.

❖ To become graceful and elegant, practice your curtsies.

WHAT YOU MAY WANT TO KNOW

❖ The origin of the curtsy was the lowering of the head to appear more vulnerable.

❖ The curtsy is also used by female performers—especially dancers, figure skaters, award recipients, and recital participants—at the end of a performance.

❖ Female dance partners curtsy before and after they dance at a very formal event, such as a Viennese or debutante's ball.

❖ The word "curtsy" can also correctly be spelled "curtsey," – its origin was the word "courtesy."

❖ Members of European courts are often greeted by curtsying ladies. Members of royal families bow and curtsy when they greet their sovereign for the first time each day.

❖ The late Princess Diana was known for her deep, elegant curtsy.

WHAT YOU MIGHT FIND HELPFUL TO KNOW

❖ The deeper, more elaborate court curtsy is used when meeting royalty in their own countries. You can sink to the floor or go down on one knee. Repeat your curtsy when the member of the royal family leaves.

❖ *The Order of Precedence in the Royal Household* is an instructional manual detailing the hierarchy and protocol of curtsies and bows in the English royal household.

❖ The famous "Texas Dip" is performed by a Texas debutante when formally introduced at the annual International Debutante Ball. An extreme curtsy, the gesture requires the debutante to cross her ankles, bend her knees, and sink while lowering her forehead to the floor. As her head nears the floor, she turns her head to avoid smearing her lipstick/makeup or soiling her dress. For stability, she holds her escort's hand.

WHAT NOT TO DO

- ❖ Stick out your behind.

- ❖ Curtsy if you are a man.

Stationery Wardrobe and Etiquette

Open me carefully.

–Emily Dickinson, Selected Letters

It looks good, it feels good, and it makes you feel special. It's civilized, courteous, and caring. It will not interrupt your yoga exercises, put you on "hold," force you to play "tag," disrupt your dinner, transmit a virus, or be received and read by hundreds of other recipients you do not know.

The handwritten note is the epitome of civilized communication and shows special thoughtfulness when used to express messages of condolence, congratulation, apology, thank you or gratitude, get well, invitation, please, and thinking-of-you. It shows extra time and care. Almost any special, private communication is noteworthy.

The Wardrobe

Your stationery wardrobe should be distinctly yours—reflecting your writing needs, your taste, and your personal preferences. Papers can be customized to match your country home, car, logo, pets, wallpaper, and favorite colors. Hand-painted beveled edges, multicolored monograms, foil envelope linings, and paper-matched inks add your distinctive touch. When selecting personalized stationery, you will choose pieces as well as consider the *sizes, weight, color of paper and ink, printing techniques and processes, and typestyle of your papers. All of these choices, of course, convey information about the writer.*

PAPER

❖ *Traditional paper is white or ecru with black, navy blue, or brown ink.*

❖ Watermarked paper ensures its authenticity. Some watermarks have become status symbols, and some are works of art. Individuals can actually have their own watermark made from their signature, logo, homestead, yacht, stage name, etc.

❖ The way to determine the best paper weight for you is to hold it, feel it, and bend it.

    o For quality letterhead stationery look for weights between 24 and 32 pounds.

    o For fold-over notes, use 64-pound paper.

    o For cards, the weight should be between 96 and 120 pounds.

    o Some stationers and engravers use "ply" to indicate the thickness of the paper (i.e., 3-, 4-, 5-ply, etc.).

    o Business and personal cards should look and feel substantial, although some prefer lighter stock because they can fit more cards into their card cases or wallet.

❖ The higher the "rag" (cotton) content, the higher the quality. The best papers are made of 100 percent cotton or of some combination of cotton, hard and soft wood pulps, and/or linen. Higher quality papers are not always entirely made of cotton, but they will have a high percentage of cotton.

❖ Recycled paper is always an excellent option, and it is available in a wide variety of weights, colors, and finishes.

❖ Handmade papers are durable, but some are bumpy and very porous. Thus, unless you prefer the "feathering" of the ink, you probably do not want to use your fountain pen when writing on them. The uniqueness of each sheet, which can include colored specks, metallic flecks, and/or particles of flowers, grasses, and ribbons, comes also from its soft colorings and deckle (feathered) edges.

❖ Whether traditional, modern, or avant-garde, your typeface patterns, type spacing, and colors of paper and ink should all blend to help create an appropriate presentation of your thoughts.

Printing Processes

Although the purchaser can choose from several different printing processes, stationery that has been engraved by hand or computer is the most elegant. This old technology for reproducing images on paper requires significant skill and experience.

❖ Embossing and thermographic printing both produce a raised surface at less expense.

❖ Flat printing, which simply adds ink to a flat surface, is usually the least attractive and the least expensive.

❖ For an unusual vintage look or special occasion cards, find someone who does letterpress printing. The oldest method (Gutenberg1455) of relief printing, the craft is experiencing a revival through the "small press movement."

❖ Engraving is the most luxurious way to personalize your papers. In addition to name, initials, logo, addresses, etc., some engrave their family's coats of arms, a sketch of a building, special flower, or animal. Although engraved stationery is more expensive than embossed, thermographed, or flat-printed stationery, the engraving plates can be used over and over again to fill many different stationery needs. The signature mark of true engraving is a slight bruise on the back of the paper, and, unlike thermographic printing, engraving is very sharp and clean. You will receive the engraving die with your first order of stationery.

❖ If you are writing with a fountain pen, select a quality water-based ink. The best inks are deep and rich in color, are free-flowing, and are made from natural dyes—some of the best are organic.

Social Stationery for Women

❖ Correspondence/Message Cards: Versatile for many uses. Monogram, name, or family crest can be used to personalize them. The border makes them less formal.

❖ Correspondence/Letter Sheets: These come in different sizes, with room to add your address, if desired. You might order additional blank sheets for longer letters.

- ❖ Informals/Fold-Over Notes/Monogrammed Notes: Usually, your name or monogram is on the front of the note, and the message is written on the inside.

- ❖ Calling Cards: Similar to business cards, these contain only personal information and are given to social acquaintances. Most include only one's name, but you can add other information. You can also write the additional information by hand on the back—a more personal touch.

- ❖ Monarch Sheets: These longer writing sheets, which fold twice to fit into an envelope, are usually used by men, but they are also used by women when writing personal business letters.

- ❖ House Stationery: This can be ordered for your country home, yacht, ranch, or estate for the use of your guests and can show the name of the property and/or just the address.

- ❖ Postcards: Some people use them for quick, simple correspondence. Your name or name and address appear at the top of the card.

- ❖ Envelopes: Look for lined envelopes.

Social Stationery for Men

- ❖ Most men use monarch sheets for both business letters and personal correspondence. They may put their name, address, or both at the top of the sheet. The use of the name only is more personal.

- ❖ Many men find that correspondence cards are useful for short personal/social messages.

❖ Most business stationery will, naturally, bear the company's logo and contact information.

❖ Correspondence Cards: These basic cards in white or ecru are an important part of a business stationery wardrobe. Use an easy-to-read and simple typeface.

❖ Correspondence Sheets/Letterhead: These business sheets should be of quality stock in white or ecru; standard letterhead size is 8 ½ by 11 inches.

❖ Business Cards: You can distinguish yourself or your business by using quality heavy card stock, especially if the cards are engraved or thermographed rather than flat-printed.

❖ Many stationers offer "wardrobe sets." This concept ensures a consistent look and a continuing relationship with your stationer. Building a set in a single-size paper family can be practical and economical.

Stationery Etiquette

❖ Fine writing accessories—paper, pens, ink, and inkwells—are still considered by many to be essential components of the well-appointed home and office.

❖ Thank-you notes should be written within a week after a dinner party and two weeks after receiving a gift. Children should be taught to write thank-you notes at an early age.

❖ You may put an end time on an invitation; this can be helpful for everyone.

❖ Using RSVP rather than "regrets only" is the more positive approach for both you and your guests.

❖ If a couple is engaged or living together, they should be invited as a pair; otherwise, two separate invitations should be sent.

❖ It is inappropriate to cancel after you have RSVP'd and accepted someone's hospitality—unless, of course, there is an emergency.

❖ You may use your calling cards as gift enclosures, but please also personalize them.

❖ Messages of condolence or sympathy should be written by hand.

❖ If a business event has more than one host, invitations should list the hosts in order of rank.

❖ Monogram manners matter because incorrect order or size of initials can be confusing to the recipient. See the Monogram Guidelines section.

❖ When a monogrammed note is engraved/printed at the top, begin writing on the first page and continue on the third page. If necessary, continue on the second page. When the monogram is in the middle of the first page, begin writing on the third page.

❖ The return address on social stationery should always appear on the flap of the envelope. You may also add name, but it is less elegant. You may use the nine-digit ZIP Code on personal stationery.

- ❖ Men who do not plan to write long letters may use half sheets. They may have a monogram, coat of arms, or name at the top.

- ❖ Always include the date—even on a short note.

- ❖ When addressing invitations use standard correspondence conventions: spell out middle names; the husband's title precedes his wife's; avoid using Ms., which is considered more appropriate for business; children over eighteen should receive their own invitations.

- ❖ Avoid using abbreviations and contractions, especially in invitations and announcements.

- ❖ When addressing envelopes of social stationery, avoid state abbreviations and write out common address words, such as Street, Boulevard, and Suite. Exclude your name from the return address. Always address envelopes with black or dark-blue ink.

- ❖ Stuff envelopes with the printed side of the stationery facing you.

- ❖ For the ultimate handwritten note or invitation, use calligraphy (even if just for the envelope)—but on simple, elegant stationery.

WHAT NOT TO DO

- ❖ Use abbreviations, with the exception of nonprofessional titles such as Ms., Mr., Jr., and Sr. Do spell out professional titles, such as Doctor.

- ❖ Write on the back of a sheet of stationery.

- Use fold-over notes if you are a male.

- Store stationery where humidity, temperature, and light are not controlled, as moisture and light can discolor it, and it can mildew. Humidity is especially a problem for the glue on envelopes.

- Use a laser printer if your stationery has been thermographed as the heat may melt the ink.

- List the stores where you have gift registries on your wedding invitations or announcements.

- Use an ampersand or a plus sign for "and."

- Use "a.m." and "p.m." on a formal invitation; write out "five o'clock."

- Send a printed card with only a printed name—at the very least also sign it.

- Use hotel stationery after you arrive home—that is tacky.

LEXICON

BOND PAPER: High-grade, durable paper stock, usually used for business letters and forms.

CALLING CARDS: Similar to business cards but with name only and used for social reasons.

DECKLE: Rough, untrimmed edge of paper.

EMBOSSING: Technique used to create raised surfaces on the paper: blind embossing is embossing without using ink; color register embossing uses colored ink for raised areas, and debossing recesses the print/design.

ENGRAVING: Traditional raised printing produced when the copy is etched in reverse into a copper plate, which is filled with ink; the engraving press then forces the paper into the cavity, creating a raised impression.

LAID PAPER: A finish that has fine lines running the length of the paper.

LETTERPRESS PRINTING: Relief printing invented by Johannes Gutenberg.

LINEN PAPER: A usually superior paper with a texturized finish that simulates the look of linen.

RAG PAPER: A high-quality paper made from cotton or linen pulp.

THERMOGRAPHIC PRINTING: A low-cost process that uses heat to create raised letters or images.

VELLUM: A somewhat translucent paper made of plasticized cotton.

WATERMARKED PAPER: A recognizable pattern, image, or design impressed on paper, which is visible when held up to the light; its purpose is to identify the paper.

TITLES, RANK, AND FORMS OF ADDRESS

Rank does not confer privilege or give power. It imposes responsibility.

– Peter Drucker

Customs vary both locally and internationally in the writing of one's name as well as correctly addressing someone with or without a title. Remembering whether to use the surname or given name first, whether to include the mother's maiden surname, or when to include the title of a foreign dignitary can be confusing for less traditional, personable Americans. Correspondence with royal family members is usually sent through diplomatic sources.

Kings or Queens

❖ In spoken address, kings and queens are addressed as "Your Majesty" (most formal) or as "Sir" or "Madam" (less formal).

❖ In introductions, kings are introduced as "His Majesty the King," and queens are introduced as "Her Majesty the Queen."

❖ In writing, kings and queens are addressed as "His Majesty the King (or Her Majesty the Queen), [Name of Palace]."

❖ In spoken address, princes and princesses are addressed as "Your Royal Highness" (most formal) or as "Sir" or "Madam" (less formal).

❖ In introductions, princes and princesses are introduced as "His Royal Highness Prince [Name]" and "Her Royal Highness Princess [Name]."

❖ In writing, princes and princesses are addressed as "His Royal Highness the Prince (or Her Royal Highness the Princess) of [Name of Country]."

Military Officers

❖ Military officers should be addressed by rank and name.

❖ Naval officers ranked Lieutenant Commander and higher are addressed as "Commander."

❖ Chaplains in any branch of service are formally referred to by their rank; however, they may be informally addressed as "Chaplain," "Father," "Rabbi," etc.

❖ In writing, always write out military titles in full.

Ambassadors

❖ Most ambassadors and ministers of a country are addressed and announced as "Ambassador (or Minister) of [Country]." Some, however, are correctly addressed with the name of the country modifying "ambassador"; these include the American Ambassador, British Ambassador, Italian Ambassador, and Japanese Ambassador.

- ❖ In spoken address, ambassadors are most often addressed as "Mr. (or Madam) Ambassador" or "Ambassador Smith." They are sometimes addressed more formally as "Your Excellency" or as "Sir" or "Madam."

- ❖ In introductions, ambassadors are introduced as "His (or Her) Excellency, the Ambassador of [Country]" or as "Mr. (or Madam) Smith, the Ambassador of [Country]."

- ❖ In writing, ambassadors are addressed as "His (or Her) Excellency, the Ambassador of [Country]."

Foreign Presidents or Prime Ministers

- ❖ In spoken address, presidents and prime ministers are addressed as "Your Excellency," as "Mr. (or Madam) President" or as "Sir" or "Madame."

- ❖ In introductions, presidents and prime ministers are introduced as "His (or Her) Excellency, the President (or Prime Minister) of [Country]."

- ❖ In writing, presidents and prime ministers are addressed as "His (or Her) Excellency, the President (or Prime Minister) of [Country]."

Foreign Cabinet Ministers

- ❖ In spoken address, ministers are addressed as "Your Excellency," "Mr. (or Madame) Minister," or as "Sir" or "Madame."

- ❖ In introductions, ministers are introduced as "His (or Her) Excellency, [Country], [Ministry Name, e.g., Labor or Culture] Minister."

❖ In writing, ministers are addressed as "His (or Her) Excellency, [Name], Minister of [Ministry Name], [City], [Country]."

Rank

❖ The rules adopted by the 1815 Congress of Vienna for determining relative rank and precedence for ambassadors and consuls are the rules that are still followed today. Washington, DC, and all foreign capitals have established principles for official precedence; and individual states and cities have their own orders of precedence.

❖ No one outranks governors in their own state except the president of the United States, and no one outranks mayors in their own cities except the governor of that state and the U.S. president.

❖ Formal dinners have their own protocols regarding receiving lines, food choice, head table seating, seating procedure, national anthems, and interpreters. In Washington, seating procedure is based on the rank of the foreign representative and seniority, which is based on the date his diplomatic credentials were received by the U.S. secretary of state. Military officers are seated by rank and date of present rank.

❖ Correct limousine order and seating require knowledge of the type of seating the vehicle provides, the ranks of the guests, and the number of guests. Jump seats can be uncomfortable for those riding in them as well as for those in the rear seat area whose legroom is restricted. The right rear seat is considered the seat of honor.

❖ A person of lower rank is always introduced to a person of higher rank.

It is an interesting question how far men would retain their rank if they were divested of their clothes.

- Henry David Thoreau

PART EIGHT

ELITE SOCIAL GRACES: THE FINER POINTS

Compliments, Congratulations, and Thank-Yous

A compliment is something like a kiss through a veil.

– Victor Hugo

*S*prinkled throughout the various subjects of this book are many common courtesies and ways of helping others to feel at ease. Lack of respect and courtesy are growing problems in many societies, but even the simplest words and gestures can help to bring about impressive change.

Everyone enjoys being appreciated, and the ability to acknowledge others is an integral part of gracious living. To give credit, recognizing, paying tribute, celebrating, appreciating, congratulating, or thanking someone properly is an excellent investment for both giver and recipient. Everyday courtesies that are effortless for us but meaningful for others are also social benefits.

The Art of the Handwritten (or sometimes typed) Note

Although letters are more personal than phone calls, e-mails, or a brief "thanks," the tradition of writing notes and letters has been compromised by the information age, and we seldom find time for it. This paucity, however, imparts even more value to the handwritten note. Don't you pay spe-

cial attention to the handwritten envelopes amidst your junk mail? Think of writing letters as opportunities, not obligations.

Throughout history, we have saved and cherished letters written by the famous and powerful who took the time to thank, commend, console, apologize, or answer a question. Think of Abraham Lincoln's letter to his son's teacher on his son's first day of school; the New York newspaper editor's famous answer to a reader "Yes, Virginia, there is a Santa Claus" in 1897; Neil Armstrong's thank you letter to his engineering team twenty-five years after the moon landing; Pearl Buck's letter of condolence to Helen Keller; and Ronald Reagan's letter thanking Americans for the privilege of being President. And, yes, real men write thoughtful notes and letters.

Although not "advanced etiquette," these expressions of courtesy will bring out the best in the recipient and you:

❖ A note written on behalf of or to a child or a pet

❖ Thank you for services or information provided

❖ A brief "excuse me, please"

❖ Holding the door open for the person directly behind you

❖ Thanks for the recommendation

❖ Recognition for your team or coworkers

❖ A spontaneous but heartfelt toast

❖ Thank you for being you

❖ Praise for good service

❖ A sincere apology

❖ Acknowledgement of a birth, anniversary, or promotion

❖ Appreciation for a party or dinner

- ❖ Thank you for your loyalty

- ❖ A smile because someone made you happy

The Perfect Compliment

- ❖ Choose the perfect moment

- ❖ Make it meaningful

- ❖ Be as specific as possible

- ❖ Acknowledge something positive about the other person

- ❖ Be authentic; do not gush.

Receiving Compliments

- ❖ Most of us find it even more difficult to receive a compliment. We brush it off with a sense of modesty—or false modesty—because we feel that by acknowledging it we are bragging about ourselves. So we react by deflecting the compliment: "It was nothing." Or by giving a compliment in return, batting it right back to the giver. When you do not thank the giver, you do not show him/her appreciation and do not permit yourself to enjoy a well-deserved compliment.

Be the change you want to see in the world.

–Mahatma Gandhi

GIVING AND RECEIVING GIFTS

The only gift is a portion of thyself.

–Ralph Waldo Emerson

Giving

❖ Everyone gives and receives gifts. Whether the giving is voluntary or involuntary, each gift must be selected and presented. And each gift becomes an extension of your taste, a measure of your interest in the recipient—even an indication of your knowledge and personal power. How and what people give make an impact and lasting impression. How the person receives a gift can be just as telling.

❖ Whether we acknowledge it or not, all gifts have meaning for those who give as well as for those who receive. They play an important role in our lives: our hunger for gifts is also our hunger for approval, affection, importance, and love—and people need to give because they need to give of themselves. Our abilities to give and to receive touch on many other aspects of our lives.

❖ The person who masters the art of gift giving will not use gifts simply to make someone feel good or to repay an obligation but will be sending precisely the message intended to be communicated, in an appropriate manner.

Receiving

❖ The receipt of a gift should usually be followed by a thoughtful acknowledgement.

❖ Sometimes "with grace" means with a smile even if it's an exceptionally ugly, unmatched pillow or you already have three Belgian waffle irons. In the interest of integrity, you can thank the giver for his or her remembrance or thoughtfulness

Gifts That May Make Cause Uneasiness

❖ A gift from a parent that makes you question your independence, especially if it is something you could not have purchased for yourself.

❖ A gift that implies the need for a return gift or obligation, which you had not intended.

❖ A gift that you feel the giver did not really want to give—or could not afford to give.

❖ A gift that you feel was given in order to demonstrate superiority or to control you.

❖ A gift that you think you do not deserve.

❖ A gift selected for the donor's own tastes rather than for your tastes or lifestyle.

❖ A gift of conscience or forgiveness—a defense mechanism.

❖ A gift that is meant primarily to flatter the pride of the giver.

In all these cases, you can accept the gift graciously if you manage to view it as a transaction that has no power over you and does not change you. Try to separate the act of giving from the specific item that is given. Perhaps appreciate the giving and consider liking the gift as a bonus.

Do not accept a present if your instincts tell you not to. The return of a gift that has unwanted sexual overtones, is a bad joke, or is an obvious bribe does not require either tact or kindness: Tact, however, is still appropriate.

Thank-you notes should be as enthusiastic and specific about the gift as possible. When thanking for a gift of money, it is thoughtful to mention how you plan to use the money, but do not mention the sum in the letter. If you have exchanged an item, thank the person for the item given, not for the item for which it was exchanged.

FLOWERS: FASHION AND FAUX PAS

Flowers always make people better, happier, and more
helpful.
They are sunshine, food, and medicine to the soul.

–Luther Burbank

I really cannot think of an occasion (except in certain religious traditions) when you could not give flowers—and neither could Emerson.
Flowers make appropriate business gifts, remember-me gifts, condolence
gifts, compromise gifts, congratulation gifts, I'm-sorry gifts, and thank-you
gifts. Unfortunately, flowers are often a last-minute gift choice, the result
of a forgotten special occasion and the convenience of ready bouquets at the
local grocery store or train station.

If this is the position you sometimes find yourself in, here are some guide-
lines:

❖ First and most important, look for quality. Select the freshest, most colorful, largest blooms. Second, remember that
the number of flowers is not nearly as significant as your
choice of flower. Third, if you are giving a small number
(under ten), an uneven number is more graceful. Finally,
one perfect single bloom (with the right sentiment) can
be simple, magical, and just as flattering to the recipient.

Gifts of interesting topiaries, miniature pineapple, bonsai or specimen trees, and herbs are also thoughtful gestures of appreciation.

❖ You also give the gift of flowers when you grace your home or office with them. Tasteful flowers and plants help guests, friends, clients, or business acquaintances to feel welcome, comfortable, and special.

❖ If you wish to send flowers for a formal dinner party, it is considerate to ask the host if you can send a centerpiece or other decorative arrangement. You might ask about colors or decorating scheme—even favorite florist—so that your gift enhances rather than clashes with the host's plans.

❖ Some special hints for the growing number of women who give fresh flowers to men: Keep it simple; give one type of flower rather than a mixed bouquet, and unless you know that he has appropriate vases and he (or you) enjoys arranging them, send them in a container. Some popular choices for men are French tulips, snapdragons (I wonder why?), and fall leaves or flowering branches such as quince.

❖ You can follow in the footsteps of many well-known persons who have delightful flower trademarks—Diana Vreeland always sent red flowers. You can make tulips, herbs, yellow oncidium orchids, colorful calla lilies, or something from your own garden your signature.

❖ Although some people do not care for artificial flowers and plants, a silk arrangement can be an exquisite gift and frequently more appropriate than the "real thing." They are especially suitable for a hospital patient when oxygen is at a premium; for someone who cannot care for plants; as a lasting memento for a mother at her baby's birth; or for a busy office area with lots of traffic. When selecting artificial flowers, be certain they are made of silk, not polyester, and check the assemblage for quality and flexibility—every petal and leaf should be carefully wired.

When Selecting Flowers for Persons Living in or from Other Countries, Do Not:

- ❖ Britain: Send white lilies, as they are appropriate only for funerals.

- ❖ France: Send an even number of flowers, which is considered gauche and is artistically more difficult to arrange; give thirteen of anything; or send red roses unless to a lover.

- ❖ Venezuela: Present unwrapped flowers; give irises except for funerals; or give red flowers unless you feel passion for the recipient.

- ❖ China: Give an uneven number of flowers, especially thirteen, as even numbers bring good luck; wrap in white paper, as it is only used for funerals—red paper is for happiness.

- ❖ Spain: Send chrysanthemums or dahlias except for funerals; send yellow roses as they mean jealousy.

- ❖ Russia: Give an uneven number of flowers.

- ❖ Korea: Send white or yellow chrysanthemums except for funerals.

- ❖ Arab world: Send flowers—usually not an appropriate gift.

- ❖ Netherlands: Send white lilies except for funerals.

- ❖ Japan: Give four or nine flowers—the word for four means "death" and the word for nine means "suffering;" you also must pay attention to wrapping and presentation.

- ❖ Germany: Give white or yellow flowers except for funerals or red roses except for romance.

- ❖ Australia: Give gladioli, as they have become a symbol of the working class and a joke—as on comedian Dame Edna/ Barry Humphries' quilted pink robe with a giant three-dimensional bouquet of "glads" embroidered in the middle of the back.

- ❖ Denmark: Give white carnations except for funerals.

- ❖ Finland: Give calla lilies except for funerals.

- ❖ Italy: Give purple flowers or chrysanthemums except for funerals; however, the luckiest number is thirteen!

COURTESIES FOR THE DISABLED

When indeed shall we learn that we are all related one to
the other and that we are all members of one body?

–Helen Keller

A ll courtesies show respect and help the recipient as well as others
to feel more comfortable. Seeing the person with a disability as a
person, not as a disability, will help you to become more aware and
sensitive.

The language that is often used to describe persons with disabilities can
be stigmatizing, dehumanizing, and condescending. The following lan-
guage is considered outdated and/or offensive and should be avoided:
handicapped, disabled, blind, deaf and dumb, dumb, deaf–mute, confined
to a wheelchair, wheelchair-bound, cripple, crippled, retarded, slow, mon-
goloid/mongoloidism, vegetable, deformed, insane, crazy, freak, psycho,
and maniac.

General Guidelines

❖ Let the person set the pace in walking or talking.

❖ Don't "talk down."

- ❖ Speak directly to the individual, not to a companion or an interpreter.

- ❖ Be patient.

- ❖ When in doubt, ASK!

- ❖ Do not pet a working dog without first asking permission, and always walk on the side of the person away from the dog.

For People with Mobility Impairments

- ❖ Do not assume that the wheelchair user requires assistance. Offer first, by asking if the person needs assistance.

- ❖ Do not lean or hang on the person's wheelchair. It is part of that person's body space.

- ❖ When giving directions, consider weather, distance, surfaces, and accessibility.

- ❖ Never push a power chair or manual chair without asking the person with the disability.

For People with Hearing Loss or Deafness

- ❖ Speak clearly and slowly, keeping sentences short.

- ❖ Do not exaggerate lip movements.

- ❖ Facial expressions, gestures, and body movements will aid communication.

- ❖ Be flexible in your language, rephrasing if necessary.

For People with Blindness or Other Visual Impairments

- ❖ Introduce and identify yourself and any others who are with you.

- ❖ Speak directly to the person, using a normal tone of voice.

- ❖ Ask the person's name and then use it to ensure that the person knows when he/she is being addressed.

- ❖ Ask the person if help is needed before giving assistance.

- ❖ Allow the person to take your arm—do not pull the person along.

- ❖ If the person wants help being seated, place the person's hand on the back or arm of the seat.

- ❖ On stairs, identify if there is a rail and ask if the person would prefer to use it.

For People with Speech Impairments

- ❖ Give your complete attention to a person who has difficulty speaking.

- ❖ Do not correct or speak for the person.

- ❖ Ask questions that require short answers or a nod or shake of the head.

- ❖ If you have difficulty understanding, don't pretend.

- ❖ Keep your manner encouraging.

For People with Intellectual Challenges or Impairments

❖ Speak slowly and distinctly.

❖ Tell the person what to do—not what *not* to do.

❖ Maintain a gentle voice and be expressive.

❖ Treat the adult person as an adult.

For People with Cerebral Palsy

❖ Interact as you would with anyone else.

For People with Tourette's Syndrome

❖ Wait for them to finish with gestures, tics, and/or vocalizations they cannot control and then calmly move on.

Thank you to the Bergen County Division on Disability Services, Hackensack, New Jersey, for allowing reproduction of some of the information from their thorough and helpful Disability Awareness Guide.

TOASTING

Here's to us that are here, to you that are there, and the
rest of us everywhere.

–Rudyard Kipling

Associated with joyous occasions, the perfect toast can set the mood *for the event and create memories for the future. Although the spotlight may be on the toaster, the focus of attention is on the person being toasted. Whether for an anniversary, birthday, graduation, retirement, thank you, housewarming, acknowledgement, wedding, or spiritual observance, the art of toasting is easily mastered.*

WHO TOASTS WHOM

* ❖ At formal dinners, receptions and large functions, the "host toasts first" rule still applies; however, at less formal, smaller, or family functions, a guest often proposes the first toast, thanking the host.

* ❖ The host is always the first to toast the guest of honor.

WHEN TO TOAST

* ❖ When all glasses are at least half full.

- ❖ If toasting at a meal, the host usually offers the toast at the beginning as a welcome to the guests. Toasts offered by others do not begin until the dessert course.

How to Toast

- ❖ Prepare ahead of time and rehearse,

- ❖ If you are delivering the principal toast of the occasion, think of it as a very short speech.

- ❖ Hold your glass by the stem and raise it to shoulder height.

- ❖ Make eye contact with the person you are toasting.

- ❖ Be gracious—the recipient should feel honored and acknowledged.

- ❖ Including a personal observation, remark, or a touch of humor usually makes for a more interesting toast.

- ❖ Keep it short, simple, and in good taste.

Receiving or Replying to a Toast

- ❖ Sit and smile with appreciation. Do not join in while being toasted.

- ❖ Always respond to a toast, if only to thank the host.

- ❖ You may then propose your own toast to the host and to anyone else you would like to recognize, thank, or honor.

Wedding Toasts

- ❖ From engagement parties to wedding receptions, there are many opportunities for multiple toasting. Sentiments should be heartfelt and specific to the toastees.

- ❖ The engagement party toasts are given by both sets of parents to the couple as well as from the couple to their future in-laws.

- ❖ The rehearsal dinner party toasts are a more casual opportunity for friends and family to toast the couple, often with personal stories. They typically feature toasts from parents to parents, parents to couple, and best man to groom.

- ❖ The wedding reception toasts are the most formal with the best man and maid of honor offering the first toasts. These are typically followed by toasts from groom to bride, bride to groom, and parents to couple.

Impromptu Toasts

- ❖ When you feel the need to offer a spontaneous toast or are suddenly asked to deliver one, remember that you need only a raised glass and a few complimentary words.

WHAT NOT TO DO

- ❖ Try to attract attention for your toast by using glassware or flatware.

- ❖ Drink when a toast is offered to you.

- ❖ Deliver a toast to yourself.

- ❖ Propose or deliver a roast instead of a toast.

- ❖ Clink glasses in an official diplomatic, formal, or business situation.

Monogram Guidelines

*A man's face as a rule says more, and more interesting
things, than his mouth, for it is a compendium of
everything his mouth will ever say, in that it is the
monogram of all this man's thoughts and aspirations.*

—Arthur Schopenhauer

A monogrammed gift is a special gift. Whether for an individual, couple or family, the present has obviously been especially selected with the recipient in mind. Because some items and merchants take longer than others to monogram, place the order well in advance so that there will be sufficient time for monogramming.

Although initials are commonly placed on silver, crystal, stationery and linens, many other gifts can be personalized, including cuff links, playing cards, luggage tags, luggage, sports implements, desk accessories, soaps, key rings, plastic cups, tote bags, doormats, leather books, shower curtains, mugs, lamp shades—even toilet paper!

Certain conventions apply to most monograms:

Style

❖ When choosing a style, consider the recipient's tastes, home décor, silver and china patterns, and lifestyle. Also consider the item to be monogrammed, the shape and amount of space available are particularly important. Design options range from very ornate and embellished to geometric and abstract. Block lettering styles are considered more modern and are also a popular masculine choice.

Order of Initials

❖ The traditional monogram is one letter—the initial of the last name; however, today's most popular monogram is the three-letter monogram.

For Individuals:

❖ When all three initials are the same size, they go in the same order as in the name. This form is commonly used on men's items, such as luggage, briefcases, toiletry bags, shirt pockets, and cuffs. When the middle initial is larger than the other two, the middle letter should be the initial of the last name. If a person has no middle initial, use a two-letter monogram with letters of the same size. If a person has two middle names, use a four-letter monogram with all letters of the same size.

❖ If a woman is married, her monogram usually consists of her first initial, her (larger) married-name initial, and her maiden-name initial.

For Couples:

❖ Unless you already know, it is a good idea to ask couples how they would like their monogram to appear. Some bridal couples create a special marriage monogram to be used on their personalized gifts.

❖ When monogramming for a couple, the wife's or husband's' first initial goes first, the couple's surname goes in the middle and the husband's or wife's first initial is last. Single letter monograms, using the first letter of the couple's last name are suitable—especially for monograms on small items, such as silver tableware. There are also some creative ways to interlock initials into a monogram.

❖ For couples with a hyphenated last name, the wife's or husband's first initial is followed by the slightly larger first letter of their last name, and then the husband's or wife's first initial appears in the same size as the first initial.

❖ When the bride does not change her name, there are two popular options: combine the two initials of their last names or use two matching separate monograms joined with a small symbol.

❖ For same-sex couples who do not change their names, combine the two initials of their surnames or use separate monograms intertwined or joined with a symbol.

❖ Do not use a married monogram until after the wedding ceremony.

Glove Etiquette

See, how she leans her cheek upon her hand!
O that I were a glove upon that hand,
That I might touch that cheek!

–William Shakespeare

Whether for fashion, fun, or freezing forecast, gloves can add that final touch to any look. Although England's Queen Elizabeth I made them fashionable for ladies in the sixteenth century, we no longer need gloves to complete a formal or semiformal outfit or to be stylishly attired. For today's fashion elite, however, they can be important accessories. Current fashion trends include many fabrics, colors, styles, and lengths. Proper fit is important in both day and evening gloves. Most gloves come in half sizes, so the perfect pair should be easy to find.

Day Gloves

❖ The classic and chic women's glove is fitted kidskin—preferably glace—and, depending on the temperature, may be lined with silk or cashmere. Other leathers, such as suede, pigskin, and patent leather may be fashionable—and more affordable.

❖ The length usually reaches to the bottom of the sleeve.

- ❖ The most elegant colors are neutral, especially black, but modern designers use other leathers, colors, and fabrications as well as embellishments to create statement-worthy outfits.

- ❖ When worn with afternoon dresses to the races or afternoon teas, short gloves of lace, silk, nylon, or cotton are appropriate.

- ❖ String gloves, driving gloves—even studded motorcycle-style gloves—impart a sporty image, while fingerless gloves, designed to keep the hands warm but the fingers free, offer an even more casual approach.

- ❖ Traditional Japanese women protect their fair skin by wearing long day gloves during the spring and summer months, often while twirling a parasol.

Evening and Opera Gloves

- ❖ For formal and semiformal occasions, the shorter the sleeve, the longer the glove. Glove length is traditionally referred to in terms of buttons—whether they actually have buttons or not: eight-button gloves are wrist length, sixteen-button gloves are elbow length, twenty-two-button gloves come to the middle of the biceps, and thirty-button gloves are shoulder length. Of course, measurements will vary somewhat according to the size of the woman.

- ❖ White and ivory are the traditional color for evening gloves; however, black can be elegant when worn with black or very dark-colored gowns. At some formal occasions, such as debutante balls and opera balls, women are required to wear white opera gloves.

❖ The actual opera glove, known as the mousquetaire, has a wrist-level aperture of three buttons or snaps that open so that the wearer can slide her hand out without removing the whole glove. Opera gloves should not be put on in public and, when removed for dinner, should be placed in your lap beneath your napkin. A glove shorter than elbow-length should never be referred to as an "opera glove."

Bridal Gloves

❖ A bride's gloves should be selected to complement her dress in material, texture, color, and design. The rules of glove length are the same as those for evening gloves—the sleeveless or strapless dress requires shoulder-length gloves, cap or elbow-length sleeves dictate elbow-length gloves, and long, fitted sleeves need short gloves.

❖ During the ring ceremony, the bride may remove her glove (giving it to her maid of honor to hold until after the ceremony) or may have the fabric of the ring finger slit so that she can remove the glove from her finger for the ring exchange.

❖ Brides usually wear their gloves in the receiving line, for formal photographs, and for their special dances with the groom and her father.

Care of Gloves

❖ The correct storage and cleaning of your expensive leather gloves is important for maintaining their freshness. When not in use, they should be wrapped in paper or cloth and stored flat, away from moisture and dampness. To avoid creasing, do not place anything on top of the gloves while stored.

- ❖ Most leather gloves may be cleaned with lukewarm water and a mild soap or a special leather cleaner. After swishing gloves back and forth, put them on your hands to rinse and squeeze away the excess moisture. Remove gloves. To restore shape, blow into each finger and lay on a flat towel to dry. Be patient. When gloves are almost completely dry, work them back into shape. To restore or maintain moisture, apply leather conditioner with a dry rag.

WHAT NOT TO DO

- ❖ Wear black or dark opera gloves with light-colored dresses.

- ❖ Wear gloves when eating, drinking, or smoking.

- ❖ Drop your glove unless you are flirting with someone.

- ❖ Allow your glove to cover the sleeve of your dress—they should meet.

- ❖ Carry or wave your gloves. Rather, place them in your purse, briefcase, or pocket after removing.

- ❖ Play cards with gloves on.

- ❖ Wear short gloves to a very formal occasion, such as a gala ball or presentation at court.

- ❖ Dry gloves near a heat source.

Old age is when the liver spots show through our gloves.
—Phyllis Diller

THOUGHTFUL HOLIDAY TIPPING

If you fear change, leave it here.

–On a tip jar

T*he expected ritual of holiday tipping need not be awkward, uncer-tain, or stressful. Because many service people with whom we deal on a regular basis throughout the year expect to be recognized with cash, determining the correct amount can be tricky. Each season brings a plethora of general guides for allocating your tip money; however, these amounts will vary considerably from community to community. And the actual amount of the gift should be determined by several factors. All tip-ping should take into account length of time they have worked for you, frequency of their service (daily, weekly, or monthly), quality of service and personalized attention, extra services they may provide, and—most impor-tant—your relationship with them. Your appropriate "TIP," a nineteenth-century acronym for "to insure promptness," will hopefully ensure continu-ing reliable service.*

Remember that, because you are expressing gratitude, a note or card is what makes your gift special. In general, cash is the most impersonal (but probably most preferred) gift, a gift certificate is more personal, and the chosen, wrapped gift the most personal. A thoughtful gift and note not only says thank you but also demonstrates that you have taken the time to know them as individuals.

Tipping Tips

❖ Make a list and create a plan of action early in the season. In a tough economy, you may have to decide which people are the most important to you before allocating your budget.

❖ Keep a list or registry of your tipping—whether cash or gift—from year to year. Although you may forget the amount, the recipient probably will not.

❖ Try to give all end-of-the-year gifts graciously in person.

❖ Present gifts of cash and gift certificates as early in the season as possible, as some recipients may be depending on them for holiday gifts or spending.

❖ Childcare providers, nannies, and teachers appreciate gifts selected or suggested by your children. These could be in addition to your gift.

❖ Gifts of food should be selected or prepared with the recipient's diet, food preferences and allergies, entertaining needs, and schedule in mind. Otherwise they will surely be re-gifted.

❖ Professionals or specialists who have done something special for you or your family over the past year would appreciate your making a donation in their name to a charity, school, or foundation that is important to them.

❖ If you would like to give more but cannot this year, do not apologize but thank recipients—in person and/or with a note. Then say that you hope to be able to do more for them next year. Or say that their gift will be coming soon, perhaps for another occasion, such as a birthday or the Chinese New Year.

❖ Some service providers may prize "good-for cards"—for future time off, a vacation, or coveted tickets to a special event.

WHAT NOT TO DO

❖ Give money or gifts to employees of a company unless you are certain that their policy allows it.

❖ Give gifts worth more than twenty dollars to postal workers. They are not allowed to receive cash, gift certificates, or gift cards. Instead give a truly special gift: a letter of appreciation addressed to the postmaster of the local office to be added to their personnel file.

❖ Give an expensive gift to your employer or boss, as this could be seen as bribery. A group gift will prevent competitive gift giving at the office.

❖ Give cash to teachers or other professionals, such as lawyers, doctors, nurses, financial planners, etc. However, sometimes parents may join to give a special collective gift to a teacher.

❖ Set up expectations for individual tipping that you may not be able to meet the next year.

❖ Present the tip in such a way that you make the recipient feel like a charity case.

REFINE YOURSELF. DEFINE YOURSELF.
THE MORE YOU REFINE YOURSELF, THE BETTER YOU
DEFINE YOURSELF

Made in the USA
Middletown, DE
22 February 2015